THE ART OF RIDING

A 'DROP' FENCE ON THE CONTINENT

The ART of RIDING

A TEXTBOOK FOR BEGINNERS AND OTHERS

by

Lt.-Col. M.F. McTaggart, D.S.O.

(Late 5th R.I. Lancers)

WITH SEVENTY-SIX ILLUSTRATIONS

ARC BOOKS, INC.
New York

By the Same Author

THE HORSE AND HIS SCHOOLING

HORSEMANSHIP FOR BOYS AND GIRLS

A HANDBOOK FOR HORSE OWNERS

ARC BOOKS, Inc.,
219 Park Avenue South, New York, N.Y., 10003
Second Printing, 1966

Copyright © M. F. McTaggart, 1951
Library of Congress Catalog Card Number: 63-12520

Printed in the United States of America

PREFACE

DURING February and March 1930 the *Morning Post* published a series of articles by me which they entitled 'The Art of Riding'. The series aroused a great deal of interest at the time, and the spare copies of the issues containing the articles were soon sold out. On this, Messrs. Methuen were encouraged to ask me to edit the articles for publication in book form. In carrying out this task I have been much assisted by the numerous letters I received from readers of the original articles, many of which expressed views that have been of great value in helping me to look at the different questions from every side. From this correspondence, also, I learned that there must be a lack of books for those who know almost nothing about horses and riding generally. Accordingly I have added to my original articles twelve sections (Part II) dealing with elementary matters; while to the title, *The Art of Riding*, I have appended the sub-title, 'A Textbook for Beginners and Others'. The result will, I hope, prove useful to that happily increasing class of persons who are about either to own or to bestride their first horse or pony.

I am much indebted to the *Morning Post* and to the Equestrian Club, Ham Common, for the help they have given me with the illustrations, and I hope that those efforts may have produced a volume which will not only interest those who are already proficient, but will instruct those whose experience lies ahead.

But to all riders, old or young, experienced or inexperienced, who are schooling horses for any purpose whatever, my advice is:

Ride with firmness, sympathy, and patience; sit in the saddle with a seat that is balanced, with legs that convey clearly to the horse your intentions, with hands that support the indications of the legs; keep the wrists supple, and maintain a sympathetic but firm contact with the horse's mouth.

M. F. McTAGGART,

Lt.-Col.

CONTENTS

ILLUSTRATIONS

* From photographs by Central Press.
† From photographs by Sport and General.

DRAWINGS

INTRODUCTION

IT is difficult to write on the subject of Riding for three principal reasons. First, because riding is an art intimately associated with the question of balance for both man and horse, and with the rules of indication, which, although of great importance and of wide variation, are often of so delicate a nature as to be inconspicuous to the student. Second, because the natural inclination of many readers to exaggerate or to misunderstand has to be overcome. And third, because fashion changes in riding as in other things, and what is accepted by one generation is laughed at by the next.

About thirty years ago it was the habit to ride with a much longer stirrup leather than is used to-day, and to sit back at every fence. Now the fashion has changed; a much shorter leather is used, and nearly every rider sits more forward over his fences than formerly. Yet the laws of balance and of motion are the same in this century as in the last.

Again, it sometimes happens that some successful rider sits in a certain manner and thereby establishes a fashion; but few can explain the reason for it.

Changes like these occur because most people are groping in the dark for a solution of their doubts and difficulties, and pursue success with an unreasoning faithfulness wherever they see it. They do not realize that it is not success alone which should induce them to change, but the realization of the dynamic principles, if any, upon which that success has been based. These principles are, of course, constant, and only await discovery and proof.

In the schooling field every rider should endeavour to find out and to practise the most perfect position for himself and his horse, so that in the rough and tumble of the hunting field he will know exactly how far from perfection he has been at each fence. Without this ideal or directing principle he will have nothing to guide him; his riding will never improve, and he will only perpetuate the faults he started with.

With regard to the Forward Seat in jumping, over which so much controversy has raged, it has often been opposed by those who say that it is practicable for the show-ring only, and not workable in the hunting field or on the race-course. Becher's Brook in the Grand National course is always instanced by the 'back seat' partisans, who show photographs of well-known jockeys sitting very far back as they land over this formidable obstacle. But such instances prove nothing. Over a drop fence the body must of course be not too far forward; the degree of forwardness must depend upon the angle of descent. If the horse 'pitches' badly, it is necessary to steady the body's forward action considerably. But if the horse lands well out beyond the ditch, the jockey is able to 'follow through' with his body, and after completing the land to carry on as if nothing had happened.

Out hunting, we have often to get over our fences as best we may. Sometimes when waiting our turn at a gap we get but little room to put our horses at the fence. Sometimes our horses are taking us too fast, sometimes too slow. Often the 'going' is deep, or we have no time to shorten our reins. But as we are not riding for exhibition, but to get to hounds as fast as we can, these considerations are of secondary importance, and if we get over a fence without mishap we are usually satisfied. For this reason there is always a variety of styles to be seen in the hunting field. And it seems to me that the style any successful hunting man may choose to adopt is no argument for or against that style, because expediency alone has dictated it.

But it may well be asked, Why have any rules at all? Why not let every man and woman get along in their own way? The reason is not far to seek. The more we study the correct seat and the right handling of a horse, the better results we shall obtain when we put our theory into practice. We shall derive much more enjoyment from riding (personally I get more pleasure out of jumping one fence perfectly than in scrambling over twenty), and there will be less risk both to ourselves and to our horses. These are ends worth working for.

In this book will be found several photographs of the 'forward seat'. From them it will be seen that it is not the exaggerated posture, unsuited to practical work, that many people still suppose it to be. It can, I think, be simply described by saying that during the parabola of the leap the rider keeps his back rounded; whereas in the old-fashioned seat he kept it hollowed. But whichever way you sit, you must always see that the knee remains pointed. On landing, the 'forward' rider endeavours to be so placed that it is unnecessary for him to let the reins slip through his fingers; the backward-seat advocate is usually obliged to let his reins out considerably. The former, also, succeeds in keeping his weight off the horse's loins, which is a matter of great importance. These are, I think, the only main distinguishing features of the forward seat; and I think if people understood it a little better, there would not be so much opposition as has existed so long in many quarters.

In other respects my endeavour is to give all the assistance I can to young riders, who, as I know from experience, find great difficulty in getting sound advice on any matter connected with horses, whether it be in the stable or in the field.

PART I

I

THE FOUNDATIONS OF GOOD HORSEMANSHIP

AS I began by saying, the art of riding is one of such subtlety and of so fine and almost imperceptible adjustment to the action of the horse, that it is a very difficult subject to treat on paper. Unlike golf or tennis, in which the method of hitting the ball can be expressed and demonstrated with almost mathematical accuracy, we have in riding the inevitable variant of the horse to deal with. This factor often sets at naught our most cherished theories, and gives opportunity for much divergence of opinion, and perhaps heated argument.

The theory of the truly balanced or correct seat upon a horse proves itself, for this reason, so elusive a subject that many instructors give up the task as hopeless, and tell their pupils that there are no definite rules, but that each rider must find his own seat according to his make-up.

With such a preliminary to equitation, the pupil may well despair of acquiring anything but bad habits, and his bewilderment is only increased when he sees a dozen riders sitting on their horses in a dozen different ways: some with short stirrups, some with long; some sitting forward, some back; some with rounded backs, some with hollow ones; some sitting on their forks, some on the back of the saddle; some with long reins, some with short; some with snaffles, some with double bridles, some with gags and mohawks; and so on almost interminably. Each rider has his reasons for his preferences, and will explain them at length, until the unfortunate beginner gives up the hope of gaining knowledge from others and starts to puzzle things out for himself, at the cost, perhaps, of a sore head or a nasty fall.

Although I fully appreciate the hazardousness of laying down rules, I feel there are certain very definite lines to work upon which must apply to all riding, no matter what the circumstances; and that, if those who are beginning to ride can get these principles thoroughly ingrained, they will not only save themselves and their horses many an unhappy moment, but will lay the foundations to first-class horsemanship. After all, we have for our guidance certain 'constants' which apply to every horse and circumstance: we have the laws of gravity and of dynamics, which are ever present and which vary in no way; we have also the action of a horse, which although it varies slightly with each animal is uniform enough to justify the framing of a few rules. It is to these 'constants' that I shall largely direct myself in the following chapters, leaving to the common sense and experience of the rider the inevitable slight divergencies caused by the idiosyncrasies of each individual horse and man.

The two photographs in Plate I—one of a whipper-in sitting at a coverside, the other of a huntsman—illustrate the diversity which exists in the seat on a horse that is merely standing still. These differences must not be brushed aside as individual questions of style of little importance. They are of the first importance. In sitting even stationary horse (unless the seat be deliberately at ease) style should always be carefully observed. The laws of balance and of control should never be neglected; for there is only one law of balance, and if it is not fully mastered at the stand and the slow paces, it is very certain it will not be mastered at the faster ones or in moments of danger and difficulty.

At this juncture I do not propose to criticize the two positions shown in Plate I in detail. I hope that when my readers have followed me to the end of Part I they will be able to do so for themselves.

II

THE SEAT: I

THE first rule of riding is so obvious that hardly anyone ever thinks about it, and few people realize its true import. It is that 'the rider shall place himself in the centre of the saddle'. Yet these simple words, obvious as they are, have so much significance that it is solely upon them and their strict application that good horsemanship is founded.

The words mean not only that the rider should sit straight on the longitudinal section, without leaning over to either flank of the horse, but straight also from the transverse aspect, so that the rider's seat rests in the dip of the saddle with a hand's-breadth between his back and the cantle of the saddle. The value of the rule does not become apparent till later on, when the importance of the balance of the body is more marked, as in jumping, sitting a kicking horse, etc.

In the early stages of riding, when the pupil is only walking, it is a little more comfortable to sit farther back in the saddle; and for this reason the habit of sitting back is not only not checked by many instructors, but is actually encouraged. Many people succeed in riding very effectively with their seats so placed, but they usually hate to be photographed in moments of difficulty, because it is then that the original error in balance displays itself.

Plate II, Fig. 1, shows a very common seat. The rider is sitting in the back of the saddle, with the feet protruding somewhat. This is a bad position for many reasons: the calves of the rider's legs are useless as aids, and the horse is generally controlled by a strong pull on the reins, the feet being used as the fulcrum.

The position in Fig. 2, another very common one, may be described as the 'hunting seat'. It will be seen that although the rider is back in the saddle, his legs are well drawn back. This is an effective seat, because the lower part of the leg can be applied to the horse's sides; but in order to attain it the stirrups have had to be shortened a couple of holes, and the knees are in consequence a little higher up than in the next photo. That is the unhappy accompaniment of this method: the higher the knee the less the control.

Fig. 3 shows what is, in my opinion, the most correct seat. Here, although the angle at the knee-joint is the same as in the second photograph, owing to the seat being farther forward in the saddle, the stirrups are two holes longer. This gives not only greater control, but greater freedom and more comfort, especially on long rides.

And there is another important advantage in this seat. It is worth, I should think, a stone in weight to the horse. For just as the infantryman likes to carry his pack high on his back, so the horse likes to get all weight away from his loins; and the more the rider can further this end the more easily will be able to carry him.

The seat in Fig. 2 is quite effective so long as things go right; its faults become apparent when the unexpected happens. If you imagine the horses in these three photographs suddenly and unexpectedly kicking, you will see that the rider in Fig. 3 will be quite prepared and balanced for the shock, while the riders in Figs. 1 and 2 will assuredly be thrown on to their horses' necks.

It should be noted that in Fig. 3 the cantle of the saddle is free of the rider's body, but that in both the other photos the whole of the saddle is filled. Furthermore, the saddle that is being used in the photographs (a pattern of my own) is made with exceptionally short measurement from front to rear; in an ordinary hunting saddle, Fig. 3 would show a clear hand's-breadth behind the seat; and similarly in Figs. 1 and 2 a little more saddle would be visible. The Italians are to-day admitted throughout the whole of the

(1)

(2)

TWO DIFFERENT SEATS

PLATE II   22

(1) A COMMON SEAT

(2) A HUNTING SEAT

(3) A BETTER SEAT

SEATS

Continent to be the finest of all riders over fences, and a prominent critic, describing their seat, said that if half the back part of their saddles were cut away they would not notice it. As, therefore, the back part of an ordinary saddle is, or should be, of little use, the particular saddle shown in Plate II has been made in order to help the rider to sit in the proper place. By this simple means, much of the effort the horse had to make when carrying a rider in the old way is saved. This is an important matter for all hunting men, especially welterweights.

When these photographs appeared in the *Morning Post* a correspondent wrote to say that the position in Fig. 3 is faulty. He submitted that in the event of the horse kicking after landing over a jump, the rider would pitch over the head because his foot was so far back. The correspondent added that the stirrup was too short to permit the rider to straighten his knees, and so absorb the force of impact on the stirrup iron. These views are perhaps widely held, and I am glad to have the opportunity of attacking them.

In the first place, my correspondent was misled by appearances. The stirrups in Fig. 3 are longer, not shorter, than those in Fig. 2; but because the rider's seat is more forward, they do not appear so. These longer stirrups are a great comfort on long hacks, besides giving better contact with the horse's side.

Then, as to what happens when the horse kicks. It is undoubtedly wrong to push the foot forward and take the shock upon the unyielding stirrup; it is a sure way to find oneself unseated. In racing, when landing over a fence, this is the reason for the leathers sometimes breaking. The force of impact should be absorbed in the muscles of the knee-joint, and this joint can come into operation only if the knee is bent, and the foot well back.

This is, I am convinced, the only position in which the rider can have complete control of himself and allow his horse to recover after a peck without interference. It is a point of great importance in the art of sitting a horse, and it must be thoroughly mastered before a proper balance and perfect control can be attained.

Some people describe this as a 'military seat', unsuited to the practical difficulties which arise when crossing a natural country. To those who believe this I reply that in riding we must think only of the law of balance, and military riding is the result of many centuries of experience. Furthermore, the efficacy of the style of seat I here recommend can be proved by examining the postures of all the most successful international riders.

There was a book published in 1717 called *The Compleat Horseman*, written by Sieur de Solleysel, who gave the following description of the true seat on a horse:

'When you are in the saddle, you must sit on your crutch, not upon your buttocks, though nature hath made them for sitting on everywhere else but on horseback. Being thus placed upon your crutch and in the middle of the saddle, advance your belly towards the pommel, as much as you can, leaving a hand-breadth of space between your hinder parts and the cantle of the saddle. Keep your shoulders a little back, and your legs straight down as if you arre on foot, and your thighs and knees turned inwards towards the saddle holding fast with them as if you arre glued to the saddle. (For a horseman hath nothing but those two, with the counterpoise of his body to keep him on horseback.) Plant your feet heavily upon the stirrups, your heels a little lower than your toes, and let the ends of your toes pass through the stirrups an inch wide or a little more: your hammes stiff and legs not too far from the horse's sides not too near neither, that is only so near as not to touch them, which is of great use for certain helps which I shall show hereafter.

'The reins of the bridle are to be in the left hand, your little finger separating the reins, and your arms pretty close to your body, but not constrained. The bridle hand just over the neck of the horse and about three fingers above the pommel, and two before it, that the pommel may not hinder the reins in their working.

'You must look a little gay and pleasant, but not laughing, and look directly between your horse's ears when he goeth forward.

'I do not mean that you should be stiff as a stake or like a statue on horseback, but much otherwise, that is free and with all the liberty in the world, as the French say in dancing "à la négligence". So I would have a man on horseback a cavalier and not formal, for that shows more a scholar than a master. Now a good seat is of such consequence as you shall see hereafter that it is one of the chief things that maketh a horse go perfectly. The very manner of sitting being almost beyond all other helps, therefore do not despise it, for I dare boldly say that he who is not *Bel homme à cheval*, or a handsome and graceful horseman, shall never be *Bon homme à cheval*, or a good horseman. And so this is enough for the seat of the cavalier.'

These rules are almost exactly what I am advocating to-day. They differ only in recommending perhaps a rather longer stirrup, and in riding with one hand. In all other respects they agree entirely.

Before I leave this subject it is necessary for me to deal with one or two other points.

There is an expression which we who have been through a riding school know well, and that is 'sitting down' in your saddle. This means in reality that the rider should sit in the saddle without constraint. For instance, no one could help sitting well in to the saddle if he took his legs away altogether. But many people suppose that 'sitting down' in the saddle means sitting well back in the rear part of the saddle, like the whipper-in in Plate I, Fig. 1.

What the author of *The Compleat Horseman* recommends is what some people describe as the 'fork' seat and liken to a pair of tongs balanced on the saddle. Naturally, this is very far from being an accurate description, but for the sake of convenience in expression I will call it by this term, in order to differentiate it from the other, which I suppose must be called the 'back' seat. The fork seat (shown very fairly in Plate II, Fig. 3) is really essential for obtaining true balance in the saddle, and for being able effectively to use the legs upon the horse in the right place. Many people find their horses will not obey their legs, and the reason is that they do not apply them correctly or in the right place. Those who sit in the back of the saddle can never use their legs so effectively as those who get 'over their work' and so use their calves upon the horses' ribs well behind the girth.

I will conclude this chapter by repeating the words of *The Compleat Horseman*:

'Now a good seat is of such consequence that it is one of the chief things that maketh a horse go perfectly.'

I urge all riders to study their seat at the walk. When this has been correctly secured, the rest of the art of riding will come more easily.

III

THE SEAT: II

IN my first chapter, when dealing with the seat, I referred only to the position of the rider's body in the saddle and that of his legs. I will now describe the disposition of the other parts of the body which are, in their own particular way, of as great importance.

The most difficult thing to teach a beginner is the correct use of the wrists. In riding, we need every joint that Providence has given us, and the wrist comes by no means last in importance. Yet we see many people who never use this most perfect of all joints, and go along as if their arms were made of wood.

Plate III shows two incorrect ways and the right way of handling the reins. Fig. 1 I can describe as the 'pump-handle' style, where the wrists do not come into play at all. Here the thumbs are pointing forwards, and the only give and take comes from the elbows. Fig. 2 shows the 'puppy dog' style. Here there is a little action of the wrist, but it is limited and uncomfortable. In Fig. 3 we see the correct method: the thumbs facing each other and the wrist so rounded that the finger-nails are visible to the rider. Here we have the greatest elasticity possible, and, in consequence, the fullest control of the horse.

Fig. 4 shows the angle of the feet on the vertical section. The leg should hang naturally, and I do not think that any instructor should attempt to alter this. If the rider is a little knock-kneed the toes will have a tendency to point outwards, and if he is bow-legged they will be much more inwards; but these differences are of little importance. The great thing is to have the leg in such a position that, without any constraint, the inside of the calf can be applied to the horse's sides.

There is a great variety of ways of holding the reins between the fingers. Some advocate having the bit rein outside, some prefer it inside. I do not think it matters much which way it is held. The best rule is to stick to the way you have been taught. Personally, I recommend having the snaffle rein outside, and always ride that way myself.

The military way of riding with one hand, on the bit reins, is to put the little finger of the left hand between the bit reins, and draw them through with the right hand until contact is reached, and to allow the snaffle rein to lie flat across the palm of the hand.

Another way is to hold all three reins in the left hand, and only the right snaffle rein in the right. Or, again, all four reins can be held in either hand, with a finger between each. The most usual plan is to have two reins in each hand: the little finger of the left hand between the two left reins, the third finger of the right hand between the two right reins.

We should not, however, follow too rigidly any rule for holding the reins. We should make ourselves adept in changing them from one hand to another, in learning how to shorten them quickly, and in changing with ease from snaffle to curb and from curb to snaffle.

We should seldom ride with one hand. Whenever we are engaged in any active horsemanship it is always advisable, and nearly always essential, to use both hands. The rein should be held at such a length that while maintaining continuous contact and control, the tips of the fingers can touch the coat buttons as the horse yields to the hand on completing each stride. For beginners, this is difficult; but it can be acquired more easily when the rider has got into the habit of shortening or lengthening the reins according to the circumstances of the moment. Before breaking into a trot shorten your reins. When increasing to the canter or gallop, shorten them still more. In each case you will find that the hands keep moving backwards and forwards slightly; and that when they are back it is just possible, if they are properly placed, to touch the buttons of the jacket.

IV

SADDLING AND BRIDLING

IT sometimes happens that the groom is away and we are obliged to saddle up for ourselves. If we have no experience we may find this a quite difficult task.

The method of procedure is as follows. First put the neck strap of the martingale over the horse's head. Hold the bridle by the head stall, with the reins ready to go over first. Then put the right hand on the horse's poll, and use the left for opening his mouth. With a little manœuvring the bit can be slipped in and the head stall lifted over the ears.

If the horse is quiet the business is fairly simple; if he is not, it may be rather difficult. He may raise his head so high that you cannot reach his poll; or he may resent opening his mouth to take the bit. Under such circumstances it is sometimes necessary to stand on a soap-box. Do not use a stable bucket for this purpose, because the horse is sure to touch it with his foot, and the noise will cause trouble.

Plate IV, Fig. 1, shows the bridle correctly fitted. Note that the throat lash is not particularly loose, its function being to keep the bridle on in an emergency. Also note the curb chain: it is hanging flat along the chin groove, neither tight nor loose. Also note that all spare links have been removed. Nearly every curb chain comes from the saddler too long, and the spare links have to be looped up in a clumsy and unsightly way; but there is no reason for these spare links, and the sooner they are removed the better. A good plan is to have six links on each side of the centre (lipstrap) link, making thirteen links in all. This, of course, refers to the large-link pattern, which is, I think, preferable to the smaller kind. But when you have to loop up spare links always remember to put the last link on first, so as to

30

(1) THE 'PUMP-HANDLE'

(2) THE 'PUPPY DOG'

(3) THE CORRECT

(4) ANGLE OF THE FEET ON THE VERTICAL SECTION

HANDS

PLATE IV   32

(1) A WELL-FITTING BRIDLE
(Note curb chain—without spare links)

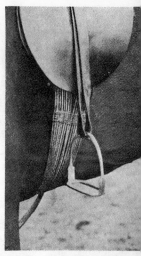

(2) TWISTED STIRRUP LEATHER

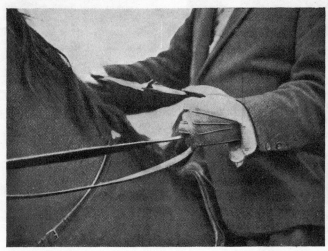

(3) SHORTENED REINS

SADDLERY

prevent the spare ends flapping about, and twist the chain in the way that makes the links shortest.

Plate IV, Fig. 2, shows the stirrup leather, which, it will be noted, is twisted. This seemingly small matter is of great importance for two reasons. First, it makes it easy for the rider to regain his stirrup when he has lost it; and unless the leather is twisted it is difficult, especially when going fast, to get the foot into the iron at all. Second, it simplifies mounting, especially with the stirrup on the offside. When mounting with an untwisted leather it is difficult to get the foot into the stirrup without touching the horse's side with the toe; this gives him the office to move off, which he promptly does, at a moment when we are not prepared. To get a horse to stand still while being mounted is an important factor in schooling, to which end the twisted stirrup leather is a great help.

Simple as the rule is, however, it is curiously difficult to get grooms to carry out. They often twist-wrist the leathers the wrong way! Of course, the correct way is to seize the strap just above the iron with one hand, and then, with the other, take hold of the forward loop of the stirrup and twist it outwards and back. It is advisable to keep the leathers on the same side of the saddle each day, because having got them into one bend it is a pity to twist them the other way.

Fig. 3 shows shortened reins. These are a great comfort. Ordinary reins are inordinately long, and get under the rider's knee or under the flap of the saddle. A good working length is 36 inches for the snaffle and 39 inches for the curb, making 72 and 78 inches over all.

I recommend this 'tip' strongly, but you will find a great many people, who have not tried it, much opposed to it. They will tell you that a long rein is essential when a horse is jumping a fence, or when he stumbles, and that unless you have plenty of spare rein you must be dragged out of the saddle. One man wrote to me to say that short reins interfered with the play of the wrists. How he arrived at such a conclusion I was quite at a loss to understand, and I invited him to come and see them used; but he did not accept the invitation. I freely admit that there are moments, of infrequent occurrence, when a horse's nose almost touches the ground, and when, if the rider is leaning back, these shortened reins are not long enough. But my answer is: When such a circumstance does arise, it is a matter of ease to let the reins drop altogether; when the horse recovers himself the reins can be picked up again without any trouble. Short reins do not restrict the freedom of head that is so necessary to a horse.

Difficulties do indeed occur in riding, but my experience has taught me that greater discomfort, and even danger, arises from getting mixed up with the customary long reins than ever could happen with these short ones. On the other hand, the comfort of using short reins is very great. When schooling a horse, and for all hacking and general riding, their advantages are so obvious that they outweigh any possible disadvantages which may be invented in their disfavour.

I will give one example. In riding, it is constantly necessary to shorten one's reins. With long reins this is always a little awkward; but with reins the length I advocate, all that is necessary is to widen the hands—and the shortening is accomplished instantaneously! This one fact alone is in my opinion sufficient to justify the practice. What happens when long reins are used to their fullest extent is displayed in Plate XIII, Figs. 1 and 3. It is because such circumstances do arise—to jockeys who sit back over fences during a race, or to hunting people now and then—that it has become the custom for every bridle to be made up in this way. But if you do not think such circumstances are likely to arise with you (and indeed I hope they will be rare) why put up with the discomfort of the long loose ends every time you ride your horse?

For polo short reins are invaluable.

V

HOW TO MOUNT AND DISMOUNT

EVEN on so simple a matter as the method of mounting a horse from the ground there are differences of opinion. In Plate V, Fig. 1, the rider is seen facing the horse's quarters. This method works well provided the horse stands still. But if he moves forward just as the foot is placed in the stirrup, the results are inconvenient and sometimes disastrous. For this reason some people advocate facing the other way, so that any forward movement of the horse, instead of being a disadvantage, is actually a help.

However this may be, Fig. 1 shows the usual method of mounting a quiet horse. The rules to be observed are that the rider should take up all four reins in his left hand in such a way as to have a firm and equal feeling upon both sides of the horse's mouth. By this means he will be in a position to check any forward movement the horse may want to make. With the right hand the stirrup should be held so as to make it easy to insert the foot, always remembering that when the rider is mounted the front portion of the stirrup iron is to be on the outside of the foot.

Fig. 2 shows the next position, in which it should be noted that the left hand is maintaining its firm touch with the horse's mouth. Fig. 3 shows the third position, which, of course, should be purely momentary; otherwise the saddle may slip: as it has in Fig. 4, where the rider has not only failed to see that the girths are tight enough, but has also pulled too much on to the back of the saddle.

The effort of mounting is considerable, even for experienced riders, especially on to big horses. For short-legged people it is sometimes an impossibility, especially with horses that will not stand still. For such as these it is a good plan to let the stirrup leather out, and so lower the iron. This is sometimes the only possible way of getting up. But if the rider is young, strong, and active, even big horses can be mounted without using the stirrup, by vaulting into the saddle. This is an excellent exercise for those who are still athletic, because it helps to supple them and to bring into play unused but necessary riding muscles.

As a general rule when starting out the mounting block is to be recommended. There are two good reasons for this. It is important to train a horse to stand still, both while and after being mounted—a difficult thing to teach from the ground, but very easy from the block. And secondly, horses, by nature, dislike having their rider on higher ground than themselves; so that unless they are systematically trained to the mounting block, they will always place themselves in such a way as to be on the upper side of a slope before allowing the rider to mount. This sometimes makes a difficult task an impossible one, and it always makes an easy one difficult.

It is rare to find a horse that can be led into a dip in the ground and that will stand there while the rider mounts from the level, but any horse can soon be taught to do this if it is trained to stand, first of all, at the mounting block. This will be found a great comfort to the rider, because after mounting it is usually necessary to pull one's coat down, adjust one's hat or gloves or reins, before moving off.

So do not think the mounting block is for elderly people only. There are excellent reasons for its use by anyone. I recommend beginners to practise also mounting on the offside. It is a useful thing to be able to do.

Before going on to dismounting I must mention one more method of mounting—the 'leg-up'. This may seem almost too elementary for a detailed explanation, but still there is a right and a wrong way of doing it.

In Plate VI, Fig. 1, the manner in which the assistant

(1) FIRST STAGE

(2) SECOND STAGE

(3) THIRD STAGE

(4) A FAULTY METHOD

MOUNTING

PLATE VI
38

(1) FIRST STAGE

(2) SECOND STAGE

A LEG UP

(3) FIRST STAGE

(4) SECOND STAGE

DISMOUNTING

places his hands should be carefully noted. The right hand takes hold of the rider's ankle firmly, and the left supports his knee. Then, on a prearranged signal (one, two, three is usual), the rider springs off his right foot, while the assistant gives a lift to the left foot. The rider is thus thrown into the saddle as shown in Fig. 2. It sometimes happens when both rider and assistant give too strong a heave that the rider is thrown over the other side. That is where the assistant's hand on the knee comes in. He is so placed that he can control the situation, and can see that the rider lands lightly and squarely in the saddle. This rule may appear to be a small matter, but if it were generally observed by grooms, to whom the task often falls, these words would not have been written.

Now we come to dismounting. In Fig. 3 we see the first position. Take the right foot out of the stirrup, place the right hand upon the pommel of the saddle, hold the rein firmly in the left hand so as to have a definite feeling upon the horse's mouth, and, as in Fig. 4, throw the leg over the saddle, just clear of the cantle, and so reach the ground. Some people keep the left foot in the stirrup until the right foot has touched the ground; others take the left foot out of the stirrup just after the right leg has passed over the horse's back, and alight on both feet at once: the variation is of little importance, and the point can be left for the individual to decide.

Another way of dismounting is to throw the right leg forward over the horse's neck, taking both feet out of the stirrups simultaneously. This is a perfectly effective way for agile riders, but when wearing a spur care must be taken that it does not catch on the horse's neck, especially as horses unaccustomed to the method sometimes throw up their heads. A modicum of risk attaches to this method, so that it is perhaps advisable not to try it unless you are supple and energetic.

After dismounting, the rider should do all he can to keep his horse motionless and tranquil. A little patting is a good thing, and perhaps a tit-bit. But don't give sugar until the ride is finished, because it makes such a mess of the bit. A biscuit is perhaps the best form of dainty. But whether the rider has anything in his pocket or no, it is always a good thing to stroke and make friends with a horse as far as possible.

VI

POINTS IN THE WALK

ALTHOUGH the walk is an apparently simple thing, there is much to practise and to learn before the pupil is fit for other exercises.

The length of the stirrup is, perhaps, the first important point. Some people, having observed jockeys riding, think that the leather should be short, as shown in Plate VII, Fig. 1. The reasons against this are two: it is a tiring position for protracted riding, and it drives the rider's weight too far back in the saddle. The position in the photograph would be correct enough if the rider were walking to the post for a point-to-point, when galloping and jumping are contemplated; but when hacking only is intended the position is unsuitable.

Fig. 2 shows the rider with too long a stirrup leather. This causes him to stick his feet out somewhat, and makes it difficult to use the calf of the leg on the horse's flanks. With a length like this, directly the rider has occasion to use his legs—as, for example, in 'reining back'—he will find his irons dangling on his toes. In this position, also, if the horse makes a sudden buck or shy, the rider quickly finds himself in trouble.

In learning to walk, there is one point which some pupils find difficult to understand. There are two kinds of walk: the 'collected' and the 'uncollected'. When riding a horse at ease, as we may after a day's hunting, we give him full rein, and let him carry his head as he wishes. This is the uncollected walk. It is a position of unpreparedness, which should be adopted only when it is pretty certain that the horse will not shy or otherwise 'play up', for if he does he will have the best of his rider, who will be unable to do anything until he has shortened his reins.

Fig. 3. depicts the balanced or 'collected' walk. This is attained by pressing the horse up into his bridle by a firm pressure of the leg, and by restraining him slightly with a delicate play upon his mouth. The unschooled horse does not, however, answer to this readily, and I warn beginners against disappointment when first they try it. The position of the rider's hands and leg should be carefully noted. The wrists are gently flexing to the movement of the horse. The reins have a light touch upon the bit, and the horse's jaw is also flexing to the feel of the reins. The leg is in the most effective position for applying the 'aids', and immediate obedience by the horse to the gentlest indication from the rider is the result. It should also be noted that the stirrup is on the ball of the foot and that the heel is well down. This is a position all pupils will do well to study. The pressure of the leg cannot, in the early stages, be maintained for long, but to maintain it as long as possible is excellent for developing the riding muscles and for learning control of the horse.

(1) LEGS TOO FAR BACK

(2) STIRRUPS TOO LONG

(3) THE COLLECTED WALK

WALKING

PLATE VIII   **44**

(3) REINS TOO LONG

(4) THE COLLECTED TROT

(1) FEET TOO FAR FORWARD

(2) REINS TOO SHORT

TROTTING

POINTS IN THE TROT

I DO not think that any pupils are fit to trot until they have not only mastered the correct position at a walk, but have also developed their riding muscles—not by the strenuous exercise of riding without stirrups or saddles, but by learning to use their legs in turning and circling their horses at a walk. I have seen beginners trotting, and even cantering, at their first lesson! What they must have suffered the next day can well be imagined. Lessons cannot proceed as quickly as that.

The main thing is to get pupils to rise from the foot. Riders who stick their feet forward have to rise from the knee, which gives that uncomfortable heaving appearance of an unbalanced body. This position I have endeavoured to show in Plate VIII, Fig. 1; but only a cinematograph is capable of demonstrating the point clearly, and the 'heave' the rider is making must be left largely to the imagination. It can be seen, however, that as the foot is forward, the rider is rising by a grip from the knee.

Another fault in nervous pupils is of trotting with the reins too short. This is shown in Fig. 2, where the rider's hands, instead of being close to the body, are stuck out far in front—a position which looks, and is, awkward.

In Fig. 3 the reins are too long. Here there is no control whatever; if the horse chooses to gallop off, there are no means, before it is too late, by which the rider can regain control. Except when we are riding at ease, we must always have contact.

Another common fault of beginners is that of clinging on with the heels. The foot is pushed too far back, the heel is raised, the toe is sunk, and the balance of the rider is thrown forward. This is a position which often puts the horse into a gallop, because he thinks, from the pressure he feels on his ribs, that that is what is required.

Fig. 4 depicts the collected trot. Here the horse's head is raised, the neck is bent. The horse is playing with the bit by flexing his lower jaw, and the rider has a light touch with the reins on the horse's mouth. The lower part of his leg is sufficiently far back to have a close feel on the horse's ribs with the inner part of the calf. This is the means by which the horse is pressed up into his bridle. Take the lower part of the leg away and the horse will cease playing with his bit and the light touch will have to go. And the position of the rider's leg may well be noted. The stirrup leather is nearly vertical. It is in this position that the best control is obtained. Directly the foot comes forward, leg work becomes ineffective.

This motion is not attained with unschooled horses, many of which have no mouths at all, and answer the feel of the reins only by setting their jaws and opposing the indication of the rider. To overcome this, much patient school work is necessary, to which many people have not the time to give.

(1) A COLLECTED CANTER

(2) THE CHANGE

PLATE X 48

(1) AN ORDINARY GALLOP

(2) HOW NOT TO PULL UP

(3) A TYPICAL SEAT

THE GALLOP (1)

VIII

A CONTROLLED CANTER

THIS pace is a very technical one. A beginner on a hired horse can have no conception of its niceties. Put the unschooled horse into a canter with an unsophisticated rider and it soon becomes a gallop; for the pace is then restrained only by the pressure of the rein, which sometimes almost reaches breaking-point. To such as these, the collected canter is an unknown pleasure.

Even with the so-called 'made' hunter the canter is often no easy matter. He may have learnt to carry the rider safely across any hunting country, to open gates, and do everything a hunter should; but when you come to a canter at a collected pace you only find resistance from his jaw, because he has not learnt to yield, to flex and to obey. For this reason, as well as for many others, I think every hunter should do plenty of school work, so as to supple his neck and ribs. It is not enough to have learnt only to jump and to gallop.

Plate IX shows two pictures of the controlled canter, and we will now examine them carefully.

Fig. 1 brings out fairly well most of the important points. The rider is balancing himself from the foot, with the lower part of the leg kept slightly back. The stirrup is on the ball of the foot. This is not, perhaps, essential, but if it can be done is a great help in giving increased resilience to the body by bringing in the action of the ankle joint. The reins, though held fairly long, have a nice feel upon the horse's mouth. The rider's hands are comfortably placed across the body. The horse is cantering well within herself, playing lightly with the bit, with a nice flexion of the neck; while the ears show contentment. The position of both rider and horse is one in which there is both control and willing obedience. Which is what is meant by the collected canter.

Fig. 2 shows the moment of change from the right rein to the left. This is not done, as one so often sees it done, by wrenching the pony over on the forehand from one fore foot to the other, leaving the hind legs to look after themselves, but by giving a slight check, so as to let the animal know what is about to happen, and then, by a firm pressure of the inward leg, bringing about the true change. This means that the hind leg changes first, followed by the fore foot. While this is happening the horse's head should be turned slightly inwards, so as to look the way it is going and in order to obtain a good flexion of the ribs. It should be noted in Fig. 2 that the rider's legs have apparently remained motionless throughout the exercise, that the shortened reins recommended in a previous chapter are being used, and that the rider is employing neither whip nor spur. The circle and change is one of the most valuable of exercises for both horse and pupil, but it takes several months of serious work before it can be done really well.

IX

POINTS IN THE GALLOP

THE gallop is a pace that should hardly be known to riders who do not race. In ordinary work a hand gallop is all that is required. In fact, the less we do of the extended gallop the better, for it puts a great strain upon the horse's legs without object or reason. As in all other exercises, there are many ways of doing the gallop, and the various seats which people adopt are interesting.

Plate X, Fig. 1, depicts an effective seat for the hand gallop suitable for all ordinary purposes. The stirrups have been shortened a little, and the rider's body is just 'over his work', the foot resting firmly on the stirrup iron. Note that the iron is beneath the *ball* of the foot. If the pupil can do this it is to be recommended, because, as I said before, greater elasticity will be provided by the ankle joint; but if he finds it difficult, then of course it is better for him to ride with the foot 'home' than to run the risk of losing a stirrup which, especially at the gallop, will be difficult to recover. Note also that the reins have a nice steady feel on the horse's mouth, and that the gallop, though fast, is not unbalanced.

Fig. 2 depicts a very common fault with beginners when they want to pull up after a gallop. They stick their feet forward to get a purchase on the reins, and then haul at the horse's head as hard as they can. This is the best way to make a horse run away. Since the feet are forward the legs are useless as indications, and the long steady pull on the reins conveys no meaning to the horse, who knows only that it is extremely uncomfortable; it is no signal to stop; it may even make him think he must go on. More accidents are due to this than to any other cause. For this reason alone many a horse has been proclaimed an incurable bolter. I think it can be stated as an unexceptionable rule that at all paces and on all occasions the rider's legs should be kept back as much as possible.

In Fig. 3 we see a rider who, although sitting fairly well, is making a quite serious mistake. Her feet are not resting in the irons, the knee having been drawn up in order to increase the grip. The fault is due to the rider's not sitting forward enough. The reins should have been held rather shorter, to enable her to get her body a little more out of the saddle. In the position in which we see her, it is obvious that there must be a very definite 'bump' with every stride. The law of riding is to keep the weight off the horse's loins, and this can only be done by maintaining taut stirrup leathers.

Plate XI, Fig. 3, shows the jockey's seat. In flat racing it has been found necessary to crouch a good deal in order to minimize air resistance. Hence, a very short stirrup is necessary. This gives the jockey very little control at the starting post; but as nothing matters so much as speed, when once he is away the advantages of the crouch outweigh the disadvantages. Yet even among jockeys we find great variety of style. Each of the jockeys in this picture, for example, is riding differently to the others, the one on the left of the picture being, I think, somewhat deservedly first.

Fig. 1 shows a lad doing a gallop in what looks a good effective seat. The toe is raised and the heel is down.

The rider in Fig. 2, on the other hand, has his toe lowered and his heel raised—a fairly common practice among jockeys. Wrong, however, because by it those important muscles of the inside of the calf are relaxed.

(1) WITH THE TOE RAISED

(2) WITH THE TOE DOWN

(3) A STUDY IN SEATS

THE GALLOP (2)

PLATE XII   54

(1) THE TAKE-OFF

(2) THE TOP OF THE LEAP

(3) BEGINNING TO LAND

(4) THE LAND

THE LEAP

X
JUMPING: I

I WILL open this chapter by tackling straight away the much-discussed and often misunderstood 'forward seat'.

Technically the expression is a correct one, but experience has shown the title to have been misleading. It would have been better, I think, to have called it 'the balanced seat'; but the accepted term came into being as a direct challenge to the old backward seat, at a time when everyone was told, even when approaching a fence, to 'sit back'. We have advanced a good deal since those days, but there are still many who both practise and teach the old form of riding.

Some little while ago I was asked to give a public demonstration of the forward seat, and because I was not seen landing on my horse's ears, some of the onlookers were quite surprised and thought I had not 'come up to contract'. In this chapter and the accompanying illustrations, I hope to make the matter so clear to my readers that this mistaken conception of the forward seat will die a natural death.

The forward seat is sometimes much exaggerated in the show ring, but there it cannot fairly be judged. The seat is a balanced one, with no extremes; a seat such as is adopted in practically every other country in the world. And the principles on which it is based are these.

When we are in motion, whether it be running, skating, riding, or any other form of movement, the line of the body must be in advance of the vertical in direct ratio with the speed and in anticipation of the expected movement. Therefore, when in the leap the horse springs from the ground, we experience the moment of greatest acceleration, and at that moment the body should be in its most forward position.

When the horse lands we experience the moment at which propulsion is least, and then the body should be in its least advanced position.

The degree of forwardness is governed by the angle of descent. When riding over a drop fence the body should not be pitched over the horse's head, but when jumping, say, open water, where the angle of descent is much less acute, the rider can, and should, keep so placed as to be nicely in unison with the horse's forward movement.

Plate XII depicts a rider jumping a simple 'up' fence where the angle of descent is fairly steep. In Fig. 1, the rider is seen using the short rein necessary for control on the approach. The hands are low, the foot is well back, so that the stirrup leather is practically vertical; and the body is raised well off the horse's loins.

In Fig. 2 the foot has come a little farther back, making the knee sharply pointed. This is an important point, because it is at this moment that the rider has to be master of his body, and this he can be only if his foot has a firm hold of the iron. He can now decide either to keep the position, as he would do if jumping a bank, or, according to the angle of descent, to retard, almost imperceptibly, the forward movement of his body.

Fig. 3 shows the beginning of the descent, when the body is beginning to rise. In Fig. 4 we see the actual land. Here the shock of impact has been absorbed in the pointed knee and in the ankle, because in this case the rider has his stirrups on the ball of the foot. In the next instant, when the hind legs meet the ground, the rider's position will be exactly the same as before the jump, the reins having remained the same length throughout.

Hence there will be no 'winding up' to do, because there has been no necessity for the reins to slip through the fingers. If such a position can be maintained when jumping, it can be easily seen that long reins are not wanted.

(1)

(3)

(2)

STEEPLECHASING

PLATE XIV 58

(1) THE TAKE-OFF

(2) IN THE AIR

(3) THE LAND

THE LEAP OVER WATER

Now, although it might seem from the photographs as if the rider threw his body forward on the approach and leant back on the land, this is not so. The body 'follows through' the whole movement with ease, and the sensation is one of being and keeping forward the whole time. Also note that the foot has never advanced beyond the girths. The only movement was when (as we saw in Fig. 2) it was slightly drawn back.

In contradistinction to this, I ask my readers to look at Plate XIII, Fig. 1, in which some horses are jumping a steeplechase fence. The 'back seat' is much in evidence. The two horses on the right of the picture have no freedom of the head; the weight of their jockeys rests on their loins; and the reins have so slipped through the riders' fingers that there will be no control on landing. This is how horses' backs are broken: if the unexpected happens they are not in an attitude to use a 'fifth leg' and will probably fall. But notice that the jockey on the left of the picture is sitting well forward, and the freedom he is accordingly able to give his horse is most marked.

Whenever you jump, therefore, whether it is in the hunting field, the show ring or the race-course, be sure to let your body 'follow through' and never, never intentionally lean back.

These photographs show clearly the conception and practice of the 'forward and backward seats'.

XI

JUMPING: II

THE three figures of Plate XIV depict a rider over open water. The angle of descent is not acute, but the horse is jumping about 20 feet in length.

In Fig. 1 the following points should be noted. The horse is taking off well away from the edge of the bank, which suggests both confidence and freedom. The animal's head is lowered so that it can see what it is doing, and it is properly balanced for the leap. The rider's weight is on the stirrups, and the body is advanced in readiness for the spring that is coming. Observe that the hands are kept low throughout; only when the body is unbalanced does the tendency to raise them occur.

In Fig. 2 the leap has been made, and the rider's body has been raised a little. But the foot is in the same position, and the reins are the same length. The horse is maintaining a flexible lower jaw. Hence the slightly open mouth. But had this open mouth been due to pressure from the reins it would have been a serious fault; there should never be any pressure on the rein in jumping. The horse must have complete freedom of the head.

In Fig. 3 we see 'the land,' after the hind legs have reached the ground. Here again the position of the rider's legs, hands, body, and the length of the rein should be noted. The rider has assumed the normal position of control, and, should it be necessary, would be ready to jump a fence again in the next stride.

It can readily be seen that the horse is thoroughly happy, not having been interfered with in any way. Remark that the stirrup has been maintained upon the ball of the foot throughout; this cannot be done unless the balance of the body is perfect. Now compare this landing with Plate XIII, Fig. 2!

Let us look more closely at these jockeys jumping the water. It is, I think, very plain that the jockey nearest the camera is definitely forcing his horse in. No horse in such a position could clear the jump, for his head is being pulled up and he is having to carry the whole of the rider's weight on his loins. The jockey next behind is in much the same position, but he is at least leaving his horse's head alone. The other leading jockey seems to be much less back, and his horse's head is properly placed: he looks as if he will clear the water with ease. I recommend a careful study of this photograph.

Looking at Fig. 3, we see once more how those who adopt the backward seat have to let their reins slip through their fingers. The 'winding up' that is necessary after landing before they can get their horses going again loses them pretty well a couple of lengths at every fence. Besides this, the extra effort entailed on both horse and rider is equal to many pounds of extra weight.

XII

JUMPING: III

IN this country, steeplechase jockeys are a law unto themselves, a law with which, in spite of the numberless falls which occur, owners, trainers, and the public appear to be satisfied. I think I am right in saying, however, that the style adopted is peculiar to British riding. If an English jockey wins several races he is accredited a fine race rider and a wonderful horseman, though the grounds for his reputation are not always apparent in these days of instantaneous photography and slow-motion pictures. Those who have experienced the rough and tumble of a steeplechase are usually the first to be generous in their criticism; they know that a camera shot at a critical moment may give to a rider the appearance of inefficiency when his unorthodox position was brought about by one of those adjustments good riding has often to make to some unexpected movement of the horse. But making all possible allowance for exceptional circumstances, I am still surprised that trainers and owners tolerate the number of falls that occur, a large percentage of which are quite unnecessary; I am astonished that they do not take the trouble to school their jockeys better than they do.

That to jump safely, horses should have free heads is, I think, a fact accepted by everyone; and yet in steeplechasing, when the jumping has to be done at speed—and therefore with more than ordinary freedom—we see too frequently the raised head and open mouth that tell their own tale.

In Plate XIII, Fig. 1, the centre jockey is in the position in which his horse's back can easily be broken. The animal's head has been pulled up and all the rider's weight rests upon the loin—the weakest part of a horse's anatomy.

PLATE XV

(2)

(1)

(3)

STUDIES OF THE LEAP

PLATE XVI 64

(1) A PRETTY SEAT

(2) A NICE QUIET PONY

(3) STIRRUPS TOO LONG

(4) THE 'BOOT HOOKS' POSITION

CHILDREN'S RIDING

In Fig. 2, the jockey nearest the camera is not giving his horse a chance to clear the jump. In fact he is doing everything possible to prevent it. In Fig. 3 we have further examples of the long rein, and of the rider's legs stuck out like shafts on each side of the horse's chest.

Falls are very frequent in English steeplechases. Looking at these pictures makes one wonder that they are not still more so. The horses certainly get little help from their riders.

Let us turn now to Plates XV, XX, XXI and XXII, which show a variety of jumping seats.

In Plate XV, Fig. 1, we have a nice free jump. The chief fault is that the martingale is too short, giving the horse insufficient freedom of the head. Fig. 2 shows a rider who, although he has been a little 'left behind', is keeping his hands down splendidly and giving his horse all the rein he possibly can. In Fig. 3 we see a little girl riding in a point-to-point, or perhaps a hunter trial. She has lost her stirrup, but in spite of that she has maintained an excellent balance, although I fear she has been somewhat assisted by the reins.

Plate XX, Fig. 1, is an example of 'hailing a cab'. The rider, however, is giving her horse complete freedom of the head, so that she is doing the best possible under the circumstances. Fig. 2 displays an unbalanced seat. The foot is forward; the rider will come down 'bump', and her reins, after landing, will have to be shortened. Fig. 3 shows a very different but equally common position. The foot is pushed well out, so that the shock of impact is taken entirely on the stirrup leather. I think that if the rider had dropped his reins he would have been over his horse's tail.

Plate XXI, Fig. 1, depicts some amateurs in a point-to-point. Two of them have definitely adopted the forward seat, and very well their horses seem to be going. Fig. 2 shows some professionals who have not adopted the forward seat. In Fig. 3 we see one rider who has completely parted company with his horse; there will be a very big bump when he lands, and at least a couple of lengths will be lost.

In Plate XXII, Fig. 1, we see one jockey who is sitting much more forward, but he must nevertheless be very uncomfortable, because he has his feet stuck out as well. In Fig. 2 we see a rider in a point-to-point riding a 'star-gazing' horse very well indeed. His position is excellent, and the way he has kept his hands down admirable. Fig. 3 shows two more amateurs sitting very well, though I should like No. 5 to be sitting a trifle more forward; as he is I fear he will land rather heavily.

From these examples, I think it is not difficult to be sure which is the right way to ride a horse over a fence, alone or in a race. The matter, however, is easier to criticize than to accomplish.

XIII

CHILDREN AND THEIR PONIES

CHILDREN are often so delightfully enthusiastic about riding that it is a great pleasure to parents to get them their first pony and introduce them at an early age to the art of riding. In doing so, there are a few points which I think all parents will do well to remember if they want that early attraction for the saddle to grow into a lifelong love of horses.

In the first place, I am sure it is a bad policy to force a child to ride if unwilling to do so. I think that the impulse should come from a real inward keenness; not from a suppressed dread, overcome by the fear of disobeying. The chance of falls should be eliminated as far as is humanly possible, even to a degree of over-caution; and when children go out hunting, they should not be allowed to get over-tired. This last point is, I think, a specially important one, because it is not very easy to carry out.

Many people suppose that unless riding is begun in early youth, really good hands and seat cannot be acquired; but this view does not bear examination, because we have so many instances of people who have begun late in life becoming excellent riders. Personally, I go so far as to say that it is better to retard rather than hasten the moment when a child begins to ride.

The choice of a pony is hardly a subject upon which much advice can be given, so much depends upon the size of the child; but it is certainly wise to try to get something not too broad, and preferably something old, quiet, and docile. Safety stirrups are also advisable, and a snaffle instead of a double bridle is simpler and easier to manage.

Plate XVI, Fig. 1, shows a little girl sitting very prettily.

Her foot is well back, and she has a nice easy balance in consequence. The little girl in Fig. 2 also has a nice seat, but not, I think, quite so good as the first, because the foot is advanced in front of the girths. The white pony, though perhaps a trifle wide, looks an excellent mount for a child, since it is obviously quiet and sensible.

Teaching children to jump is often very difficult. It is important to have a pony which, without rushing or jumping too big, jumps freely. If a pony refuses it isn't easy to get it jumping without a bit of 'smacking', which is bad for the pony and teaches the child a wrong lesson. Under such circumstances, before asking the child to get up, the pony had better be longed over several times, until it has given up the practice of refusing.

Needless to say, the jumps should in all the early stages be very small indeed; it is better for the child to ask to have the jumps made bigger, than that there should be any dread of jumping an obstacle which appears formidable.

If the child is very small there isn't much instruction that can be given, and if the fence is negotiated without mishap, that is as much as can be expected. But with older children (and jumping should, I think, not be started till a child is fairly big), it is important to see that they do not get into bad habits of style, because these will be so much more difficult to correct in after years.

In Plate XVI, Fig. 3, we see a little girl who has been allowed to jump without shortening up her stirrup leathers, and all her faults in pose are due to this. But the way she has managed to give her pony its head and keep her hand low, instead of clutching the reins and jabbing the animal in the mouth, is very good.

In Fig. 4 we see another little girl, who is in what is called the 'Boot Hooks' position: that is, the attitude we adopt when pulling our boots on in the morning. She is being carried over the jump by the reins, and the pony has no freedom for its head. This is a practice that should be checked at once, because it is an easy habit to get into and a difficult one to get out of.

It goes without saying that children should never be allowed to ride in spurs. I think nothing looks worse; but I fear some have an idea that spurs look smart. It should be our endeavour to explain that it is always possible to get things done by kind methods. It is not pretty to see children being taught to give their ponies 'big whacks' when they jump, instead of to use the more effective and pleasanter methods of patience and gentleness, combined with quiet determination.

A very good way of teaching children to sit over fences is to make them catch hold of the neck strap of the martingale. This not only gives confidence, but it prevents any jabbing of the pony's mouth. As the child gains experience, the strap will be required less and less, until the correctly balanced seat is permanently attained.

Never forget that to a child a fall can be a serious matter, and, if it be a painful one, may have very far-reaching effects, sometimes affecting the nerve so much that the child can never face a horse again.

Therefore, 'safety first' must be the motto all the time.

XIV
THE SIDE-SADDLE

WHETHER women should ride astride or on the side-saddle is a question at present undecided. The supporters of the side-saddle are staunch in their adherence to it and indignant at any suggestion of change.

The whole controversy can, I think, be summed up in a few words. With provincial packs, and for hacking, when there is comparatively little galloping and jumping, women can very well ride astride, because the effort is not too great. But the side-saddle is undoubtedly easier, and in the Shires, where there is frequently galloping over ridge and furrow to do, and fences to negotiate that would tire a man hardened to long hunts, I think there are many ladies who find the strain too great for cross-saddle work, and who, for other reasons, will always favour the old-fashioned way. This applies especially to those who have so many other calls than hunting upon their time that they have few moments left in which to study and practise the cross-saddle method.

The side-saddle, however, is a cumbrous thing. It weighs a great deal, it has usually to be girthed and strapped very tightly, and unless it is frequently restuffed and carefully fitted, sore backs are likely to arise. But even if the saddle fits well, unless the rider knows how to sit on it the fateful sore will sooner or later be found. On this point grooms want watching. They know that it will be unpopular to point out the rub, and accordingly they tell the owner that all is well and turn the horse out on the next hunting day with the sore well hidden under the saddle. Every lady should therefore make it a rule to look herself at her horse's back every time she comes in from riding. If

(1) SITTING CENTRALLY   (2) SITTING ASKEW

(3) STIRRUP TOO LONG   (4) CORRECT LENGTH

THE SIDE SADDLE

PLATE XVIII   72

(1) FOOT TOO FAR FORWARD

(2) THE WALK (CORRECT)

(3) TROTTING (RIGHT SHOULDER FORWARD)

(4) THE CANTER (CORRECT)

THE SIDE SADDLE

this were systematically done, many an incipient sore would be checked in time.

There are two distinct types of side-saddle, necessitating very different methods of riding. In these articles I propose to deal chiefly with what is known as the 'forward seat' saddle, which is the one, I think, most popular to-day.

The first thing is to learn to sit square on the horse's back. Plate XVII, Fig. 1, shows the correct position, where if the seam of the coat is projected downwards it runs over the horse's dock. Fig. 2 shows a common fault with beginners: the seat is over on to the offside, and the seam of the coat is well away to the right. This fault is often due to the top pommel being placed in an incorrect position for the particular rider.

Figs. 3 and 4 show the length of the stirrup and the position of the legs. Fig. 3 shows the rider with an almost straight leg. This brings the right shoulder round, and puts too much weight on to the near side. The stirrup should be short enough to enable the rider to press the thigh against the leaping, or lower, pommel when required. In ordinary riding there should be nearly the space of a hand's-breadth between it and the top of the rider's leg. Fig. 4 shows the correct position fairly well. Here the stirrup is the right length, so that the upper part of the thigh is well away from the pommel, and the left leg is in exactly the same position as when riding astride.

Now we come to the side-saddle seat on the move.

In Plate XVIII, Fig. 1, we see the result of having the right foot too far forward: the whole weight of the rider is brought on to the back of the saddle, which is, of course, the wrong place for the horse to carry it. In this position, any sudden movement of the horse will find the rider 'left behind' without hope of immediate recovery. The second photograph shows the correct position of the legs at the walk, with the rider sitting straight and square.

In Fig. 3 we see the effect, at the trot, of bringing the right shoulder too forward. This makes the whole position uncomfortable, and the 'screw' of the rider's body as she rises and falls in the saddle is a sure forerunner of a sore back. In Fig. 4 (at the canter) we can see the difference at once. The rider is sitting square on the saddle, as in the trot. It is unnecessary to grip hard on to the pommels when the body is in the right position; grip—as opposed to the *pressure* which must always be used—should, after all, be necessary only to correct a balance that is becoming unstable; it is not required to maintain one that has been properly gained.

The spot on the back where a horse most easily gets a sore is on the off wither, due to the rider's having sat with a practically straight leg; the correct balance being thus lacking, all the weight is taken on the stirrup iron and the saddle made to press into the off side of the wither. Directly the horse begins to trot or canter this causes a movement of the back of the saddle which soon rubs a hole in the horse's back close to the backbone.

Many ladies still advocate riding in sharp spurs, but the majority, I think, prefer blunt ones. Personally, I think it much better to have no spur at all and to ride with the bar heel. For side-saddle riding the reins should be about 4 ft. 10 in. in length.

If a horse has not been accustomed to the side-saddle, or has just come in from grass, care should be taken to see that his back is hardened first, by keeping the saddle on in the stable for an hour or two each day and applying hardening lotions. In fact, whenever the side saddle is used the horse's back must be the primary consideration.

XV

SOME OPINIONS

ALTHOUGH we have been a nation of horsemen for many centuries, there has never yet existed a central school from which new ideas could radiate. The result is that riding is often picked up from grooms or local riding masters whose qualification to instruct is nothing more than that they have ridden longer than their pupils. Hunting men, who ride regularly to hounds and were originally taught upon hunting lines, become set in their habits and feel a somewhat natural resentment if it is suggested that their early teaching was incorrect. It is therefore no matter of surprise to find experienced riders possessing different views from those I have advocated in the foregoing chapters. When these chapters appeared as articles in the *Morning Post* I received a large number of letters; the questions they raised, often very interesting, gave me the opportunity of explaining or enlarging upon points which were either obscure or contentious. In this chapter I propose to deal with some of those questions.

Perhaps the most controversial matter of all is the correct seat on a horse, chiefly because it is seldom examined in detail or worked out to a logical conclusion. Many instructors are content if the rider sits the horse without falling off, and evade awkward questions by leaving the pupil to adopt his own style. In my young days, though in a military riding school, I was never taught any details of the seat; as long as I could see only an inch of my foot as I sat in the saddle, and held the reins correctly, nothing else mattered very much.

Hence, it can readily be seen that any author who makes the attempt to give those very definite instructions that are essential to true and accurate balance in the saddle, will at once meet with many conflicting opinions.

One correspondent very strongly deprecated keeping the knee pointed, telling me that the correct seat is one in which the lower part of the leg is pushed forward towards the horse's shoulder. To support this contention the Elgin Marbles were instanced as representing the real seat on a horse. In case this argument appeals to some of my readers, I must state that in the statuary, the figures ride without stirrups or saddles, and the attitude adopted is totally different from the one we, with both saddles and stirrups, use to-day. If we stick our feet forward when riding in stirrups, we push our body backward, and the absurdity of this is apparent to anyone who pauses to consider the first law of movement: to be in advance of your work.

Another moot point was the disposition of the weight on the iron. Throughout the preceding chapters I have advocated the rider's keeping a taut stirrup leather and balancing himself from the foot. Here again I met with opposition, but this time it was due, I think, to the difficulty of expression, not to a real divergence of opinion. Some people suggest that if you balance yourself entirely from the foot you become perched in the air and ride as if you were a pair of tongs, an argument which produces the tenet that the rider must balance himself from the knee. To this I am much opposed. If you teach a rider to balance from the knee, you teach him to become constrained and to think that the first law of riding is to maintain an iron grip. And not only that: if you think it out carefully, you will realize that it is not possible to remain definitely balanced from the knee for more than a few seconds; it is much too exhausting. Again, some correspondents suggested that if a pupil were taught to balance himself from the foot he would undoubtedly fall off if a stirrup leather were lost. This, of course, is nonsense. If a rider has his weight largely on

(1) COLONEL BORSARELLI (ITALY)

(2) LIEUTENANT DE BREUIL (FRANCE)

THE CONCOURS AT ROME

PLATE XX 78

(1)

(3)

(2)

STUDIES OF THE LEAP

the iron it means he is balanced, and a balanced rider can surmount any difficulty that arises. Grip is not a thing to teach; grip comes naturally, without instruction, provided the rider is properly placed in the saddle.

Many people advocate riding with the stirrups home. This is not a very important point, and if you like to ride thus there is no great harm in it. But I must point out that by so doing you lose all the extra spring of the ankle joint. Personally, I think the feel of landing over a jump with your stirrups on the ball of the foot is very preferable to that of landing with them home; but it is not so easy to do, and if you are a beginner it is better to ride in the way that comes easiest.

Another writer suggested that if the lower part of the leg is drawn back, the knee itself cannot get close into the saddle, and what he described as 'the fatal triangle of light' appears. This is a very curious idea. There is nothing fatal or even wrong in bringing, when at the walk or stand, the inside of the knee slightly away from the saddle. The really important thing is to have the muscles of the inside of the calf close to the horse's ribs. Directly the horse breaks into the trot or canter, I can assure any readers who think like this correspondent, the 'fatal triangle' disappears at once, and the knee takes up its function of holding firmly to the saddle.

The view I have already referred to, that, if you have your leg back, when the horse kicks you will be thrown over its head, cannot be taken seriously; but I mention it because it is an opinion which I know is definitely held by a well-known riding instructress!

The angle of the lower part of the leg is another bone of contention. Some people say that the shin-bone should be vertical with the ground. This position has two faults: in the first place it puts the rider too much back in the saddle, and in the second place it does not permit the inside of the calf to press against the horse's ribs.

The last point I propose to deal with is, once more, that of the forward seat.

I think I have shown clearly in Chapters XI to XIII that the forward seat can be adopted at all paces. But in order to give the point a final proof, I submit in Plate XIX two photographs showing a Frenchman and an Italian jumping in the concours in Rome. It may not be generally known in this country how supreme the Italians are to-day in all matters connected with cross-country riding. The course they have every year in Rome is the most difficult in the world. Yet the Italians do not ride expensive horses. But they train and ride their horses so well that they have proved themselves practically unbeatable. The fence shown in Plate XIX was a particularly big one. It consisted of $15\frac{1}{2}$ feet of open water, with a triple bar in front 5 feet high and 8 feet in width.

Now let us examine the two riders. The Frenchman (Fig. 2) is forward, but not forward enough, and the result is obvious: he will not get over.

The Italian is well forward, helping his horse in every way by not hindering his movements: and he is clearing the fence perfectly.

I should add that the Italians ride very fast at their fences, so that the difference between their galloping style and steeplechasing, although distinct, is not very great.

These photographs are well worth careful study. And remember that when a horse is making a supreme effort the rider must be in a correspondingly extreme position.

PART II

XVI

EARLY LESSONS

I HAVE often observed how instructors seem to think the best way to teach riding is to make the lessons as difficult as possible. They make their pupils ride in early stages without stirrups, and even (especially in military riding schools) without saddles. The idea is, of course, to develop the pupil's grip, to give him balance, to 'stretch' his muscles, and to get him what is called 'down in the saddle'.

These methods are prevalent, and it is hard to get them altered. But they are wrong, and the sooner they are altered the better it will be for the standard of English riding. For in the first place muscles cannot be 'stretched'; they can only be suppled. In the second place, riding without stirrups gives the pupil a wrong impression of what balance really is; he learns to keep his balance by gripping hard, and as he cannot use his feet for this purpose his line of equipoise becomes distorted. And in the third place, the best way to get a rider 'down in the saddle' is to instil confidence in him; when a pupil is not 'down' the reason is that, from lack of confidence, he is not sufficiently relaxed, and he is hardly likely to relax by being made to trot round without his irons. For these reasons riding without stirrups does, in my opinion, not only no good but actually retards progress. I have also observed of instructors that when teaching jumping they frequently insist on their pupils going over a fence without reins. This again is making the lesson difficult without adequate reason. The pupil must, of course, learn to jump without pulling at the horse's mouth, but making him cross his arms while jumping will certainly not teach him to do this.

The great thing in jumping is to keep the hands 'down and out', and it is upon this point that the instructor's attention should be directed. An easy way is to make the pupil hold on to the neck strap and continue to jump over a small fence until he can do so without the strap's assistance. There are several advantages of this simple method. The horse can jump with the certainty of having his mouth not interfered with. The pupil gains confidence and in a very short while can concentrate on the 'down and out' rule, which under other circumstances he would find difficult. By this means, also, he is taught to keep his hands and his body in the right position, and not, as happens when he is made to cross his arms, in some quite other place. Those instructors who get their pupils to jump without reins or stirrups have mistaken their role: they should be teaching trick riders for a circus.

In every subject but riding, beginners are taught to start from the beginning and to work by easy stages to more difficult matters. Yet riding can be no different in this respect from any other accomplishment. Obviously it should be the aim of every instructor to discover how he can make his lessons *easy*. It is ridiculous of him to ask his pupils to do things which even he himself would find uncomfortable and distasteful.

To those, therefore, who undertake the difficult task of teaching riding, I submit the following method for consideration.

And first it must be borne in mind that the riding muscles of one who has never crossed his legs over a saddle are extremely weak, and the skin on the inside of the knees is easily chafed. Therefore begin with light work. It is much better for a pupil to progress slowly without a check, than for him to do a lot of work on one day and to find himself too sore and stiff to ride at all on the next. For all but very athletic pupils, ten minutes in the saddle at the standstill is sufficient for the first lesson, and fifteen will be ample for the second. After that the lessons can be rapidly lengthened.

The best of all methods of teaching riding is with a wooden horse. Let a pupil use this and this only for the whole of the first week's instruction. If a wooden horse is not procurable, the next best thing is a very quiet old horse that has learnt to stand perfectly still. It is astonishing how much can be taught in this way and what progress can be made in a few lessons. The pupil gains confidence; he gets to know the feel of a horse from the saddle; and he develops necessary riding muscles without danger of sprain or fall.

From this point the number of things that can be taught is large:

1. Mounting and dismounting.
2. The correct seat in the saddle.
3. How to hold the reins.
4. How to shorten the reins.
5. How to shorten or lengthen the stirrup leathers from the saddle.
6. How to tighten the girths.
7. The practice of the correct grip.
8. Suppling exercises of the back and arms.
9. The names of parts and fitting of saddlery.
10. The names of the parts of a horse.
11. How to describe a horse.
12. Simple veterinary matters.

All these important matters can be taught indoors if the weather is inclement. In my opinion a beginner can spend his first week in no better way.

In the second week he can start upon the walk, putting into practice what he has learnt during the first week. He must be made to use his legs constantly, because unless his riding muscles are strongly developed he will never be able to ride well. Let him try to do the half passage, right or left shoulder in, etc.; show him the turns, forehand, centre and lock, and make him try to do them. He will not, of course, be successful to begin with, but that is no matter; he will be doing what is very important—developing his muscles and learning that there is a great deal more in the art of riding than he ever imagined.

After this the pupil may begin to do some trotting. The canter should not be dreamed of until the trot has been fairly well mastered.

If this plan is carried out, I am convinced that in a short time a pupil will be more advanced than he would be if taught by any other method. For he will not have wasted a moment upon tasks he is unlikely to attempt after finishing his lessons. Nor will he have experienced a single hour's discomfort from stiffness, sprains, or chafes. Above all, his confidence will have steadily grown.

XVII

STABLE MANAGEMENT

THE first principle of stable management is this: 'Treat a horse as you would treat yourself.'

This simple rule is the key to a great variety of perplexing matters and the solution of many problems. It is a rule that enables one to silence, or at least to cope with, the loquacious groom who, having 'been with horses all his life', thinks he knows all there is to know, and who, in consequence, does a great many things in which there is no sense and no reason. It is a guiding principle that ensures your horses being treated on lines which can never harm and may do a great deal of good. It is so important that it should be pinned to every stable door. 'Treat your horse by the same rules that you apply to yourself.'

With this for text, let us now see how it applies, and what it will enable us to avoid.

Feeding.—Man has been given a small stomach; he requires at least three meals a day, and rather likes four. The horse also has a small stomach, and he too must have at least three meals a day, and preferably four. Luckily for our pockets, however, it is not necessary to vary the food of a horse to the same extent as we vary our own. A horse is content with hay, oats, and bran for every meal, and a linseed mash on Saturday night; and perhaps, if it is doing very hard work, a few beans can be added, just as an athlete can eat a mutton chop for breakfast.

The amount a horse eats depends upon his size, and the work he is doing, so that we cannot lay down a fixed schedule. We must use our discretion. But we can base our decision upon the fact that a horse of about 15 hands, doing two hours work a day, should have about 10 lb. of oats and 12 lb.

of hay every day. To this we should add about a couple of
pounds of bran, which, although in these days of steam
milling without much nutriment, gives bulk to the feed.
Rock salt should always be either in the manger or hung on
the wall as a 'lick'. On Saturday night the linseed which is
given instead of oats should be well boiled beforehand, so
that it is served as a jelly and not as hot seeds.

A horse in good health that doesn't eat his feed is probably
telling you that there is something wrong with the forage,
or perhaps with his teeth or gums. You must think what
the reason can be. If he is constipated, a dose will help.
If he has got a chill, look out for draughts, and see that he
is thoroughly warm. But often enough, lack of interest in
the manger is due to bad forage. The bran may be sour,
the hay may be musty or of bad quality. Learn to know
good hay from bad. Good hay smells sweet and nutritious;
it should be firm and free of weeds. Bad hay is soft, with
little smell, like the stuff used for packing. The bran should
be clean and smooth, with large flakes, and floury to the
touch. The oats should be hard, and free of weevil.

So much for the dietary of a horse. The times of feeding
are much the same as for our own meals: breakfast, dinner,
tea, and supper. The subdivision of the feeds can be left
to your discretion.

The position of the hay rack used, in old-fashioned
stables, to be high up over the horse's head. Nowadays it
has been found better to leave the hay on the ground, which,
after all, is the natural place for hay. Many people go so far
as to advocate feeding horses entirely off the ground, and
their view has much to recommend it.

Ventilation.—The stable must be both light and airy.
Don't allow the groom to close up all the doors and windows,
and so keep the horses unnaturally warm. This applies
especially to the night-time, because closed stables produce
such an atmosphere of ammonia that the smell becomes

stifling. This is particularly noticeable when entering the stable in the early morning. The test of good ventilation is that the stable should be not only fresh, but also not too cold. Nevertheless, a cold stable is better than a stuffy one. Bad ventilation breeds coughs, which are often very difficult to cure.

Companions.—Horses are by nature gregarious, and I am much opposed to the lonely horse-box. Let a horse have some sort of companion, though it be only a goat. Lonely horses often fall into bad habits, such as crib-biting or wind-sucking, for no other reason, I am sure, than that they are bored to death.

Rugs.—Once again, common sense should be your guide. In warm weather no rugs are required, but their place should be taken by a summer sheet to keep the flies off; in mild weather one rug is sufficient; in really cold weather three may be necessary. Simple rules, but very seldom strictly carried out! Grooms often have their horses heavily rugged up day and night in all weathers. It is usually better to under- rather than over-rug, because the constant weight on the horse's back causes a sore on the wither, which is unsightly as well as difficult to cure. Let us remember that we should not ourselves like to wear heavy overcoats all day long in the house.

Cleanliness is, naturally, another essential to good horse management. But as even this is not always thoroughly attended to, let us go over the points that should be emphasized. All droppings must be removed at once, before the horse has time to tread them into the bedding, or get them into his feet. Lazy grooms are apt to overlook this. To keep a horse healthy, he should be groomed thoroughly once a day. If this has been done properly, you should be able to run your fingers through the coat and find no dirt or grease left upon them. When grooming a horse, the important parts to sponge out are the eyes, the nostrils, the dock and sheath; and the important parts to dry are the loins, the chest, the throat, and the heels. The feet should be carefully picked out and washed.

Watering.—Once more, our rule applies. The circumstances under which we want a drink, and what we do to quench our own thirst, hold good with a horse. Keep water permanently in the boxes or stalls, and let your horses drink whenever they are thirsty. Only be careful they have not had a feed of corn immediately beforehand, or that you do not want to gallop them immediately afterwards. That is all that matters. You will soon find, however, that this rule for watering is not one upon which people are by any means unanimous. Grooms, and many owners, have all sorts of strange ideas, and keep their horses waiting for water for a variety of reasons, none of which, I venture to affirm, is sound. Even experienced people have curious notions on this point.

Their reasons are mostly connected with colic. Many people will not let a horse water when coming home from hunting for fear of bringing on this complaint. But if they understood what colic really is, and how it is brought on, they would soon drop all their restrictions and allow their horses to drink like human beings. The true explanation of colic is simple. The horse differs from the camel or the ox in having a small stomach. When he is thirsty he can soon fill it to overflowing. A thirsty horse can drink two bucketsful of water—far more than his stomach can hold —and the water then runs into the intestines. Now, if the stomach is full of undigested corn, it is quite possible that a few whole oats may be carried down into the guts, and so cause the intense pain known as colic. But if there are no undigested oats in the stomach, then colic, from drinking water, cannot occur.

Thus we see that the only thing we have to avoid is feeding a thirsty horse before letting him drink; and as we are not likely to do such a thing, we can definitely turn down all the odd notions that grooms and others hold on this subject. Horses certainly do get colic, but from other causes.

Horses sometimes break out over and over again into a sweat after they have been groomed. Many grooms attribute this to water, and reduce the allowance accordingly. But, again, it has nothing to do with watering. It is due to purely nervous excitement, and the cure is to see that your work is of a less exciting or exacting nature.

So let us have our watering rules firmly fixed in our minds, and not let anyone talk us round. When out riding, if we let the horse drink, we must be careful not to gallop him immediately afterwards, or to let him stand at cover side in the cold for too long, for either may give him a chill. But, after all, these are rules which would apply to ourselves, and we should treat our horses in the same way.

Exercise.—To keep a horse in the best condition, he should do two hours good work a day. That is the happy mean, which we should use as a guide. More than that, during day after day, may easily be too much; less than that is too little.

If we are hunting, this rule should especially be our guide in deciding what a horse should do and can do. The fact that strong horses of the right age, if they are not called upon to carry too much weight, can do an immense amount of work, may make us deceive ourselves. Any horse that has carried a man to hounds for six hours (door to door) has had enough. That he can apparently do more and not seem tired, is liable to mislead us, making us think he can do much more. But his spirit does not reach to his legs, and when a horse has done too much the fact will be proclaimed next morning by his hot and puffy legs. It is wiser, therefore, to hunt less long and more often, than to overtire a horse each time you take him hunting. I know cases of horses that get practically no exercise for six days of the week, and then are taken out for a long day on the seventh. Under such treatment no horse can remain sound for long.

Watch your horse's forelegs as you would study a barometer. They give the signal for the amount of work that is necessary each day. Because puffiness decreases after a little exercise, that does not necessarily mean that the work is doing them good. A puffy leg is usually nature's call for decreased work. I use the word 'usually' because sometimes a horse is liverish from not doing enough work, and the legs fill for that reason; but this is easy to discover and remedy.

A great many hunters are overworked; which is why so many are unsound, and are sold to knackers as useless before they have reached even the prime of life. The horse has a wonderful generosity, and will give all he has to give, and it is up to you to see that you do not ask too much. Be generous, too.

Shoeing.—Horses should be shod once a month. To ensure that your horse has been properly shod, look to the following points:

1. That the shoe has been made to fit the foot, and not the foot to fit the shoe.

2. That the frog touches the ground.

3. That the shoe lies flat on the foot and does not pinch the heel.

4. That the hoof has not been too much pared away. Corns and other lamenesses arise from the contraction of the heel, and we should be particularly careful that the V-shaped frong has plenty of room for expansion.

Clipping has to be done every winter. The first rule is to clip during the last week in October and the first week in December. By so doing only two clips are necessary. But if you have plenty of grooms, with every convenience, you can clip whenever you think necessary, winter or summer. For hunters, it is best at the first clip to leave the legs; but clip all over for the second clip. Never, at any time, leave a saddle-mark.

Bedding.—The best bedding is good wheaten straw, but it is more expensive than other kinds. If you can't run to it, don't buy cheaper stuff—such as oaten straw, which, being more wasteful, is no cheaper in the end—buy peat moss. It isn't so pleasant in appearance, but it makes an excellent bed, especially if mixed with sawdust.

Bandages.—A very vexed question! Here again, I beg of you to act upon the rule of treating your horse as you would treat yourself. If you swathe your own ankles and wrists in damp bandages all day long because you think it strengthens them, then I suppose it is logical to do the same to your horse. But if you don't follow this principle for yourself, why put bandages on your horse? Bandages, of course, have certain definite uses: for warmth, for keeping on cotton wool over a cut, for protection while travelling or perhaps racing. But they will not reduce swelling, which responds only to massage. Most grooms love to put on tail bandages, because it looks as if they were very thoughtful, and because at the same time it saves them the trouble of cleaning. It has accordingly become a very prevalent practice. I consider tail bandages do more harm than good. It is only necessary to see that the roots of the tail are well cleared (never use a comb), and perhaps the hairs smoothed down with a water brush. I never allow bandages on any of my horses, except for the very definite purposes I have mentioned.

In *Grooming* observe the following rules:

Early morning: a rub over to clean away all dirt acquired during the night.

Immediately after exercise: thorough grooming. Never allow a horse that has come in hot to remain undried. If this cannot be avoided, put on bandages and rug up, or have the animal walked about till cool. Dry the extremities first. Don't remove the saddle and expose the heated skin too quickly. Water should be used to remove dirt only, not to clean the coat. The legs should not be washed; they should be dried with straw; water is liable to bring about mud fever, unless dried off immediately after.

Evening: a good wisping is excellent. This is not so much for cleanliness as to produce a good shining coat, and to massage the muscles.

Finally, be *quiet*. A noisy groom is a bad groom. Never shout at your horses in the stable, or handle them with roughness or impatience.

With these simple rules any stable can be run efficiently. But you will find that my golden rule—treat a horse as you would like to be treated yourself—is at present far more honoured in the breach than in the observance. In carrying it out you will have to be very firm with your groom, who will probably oppose you to the limit of his capacity. But pay no attention. Be determined that you will frame your stable rules upon this principle, and you will soon be rewarded by the healthy and happy condition of your horses.

XVIII

COMMON AILMENTS

LAMENESS.—The golden rule for preventing lameness is never to ride a horse when he is tired. When your horse has had enough, go home. But this, I know, is not always easy to do, and sometimes is impracticable. Nevertheless, the theory is sound, and should be observed whenever possible.

As I have said in a previous chapter, the condition of the fore legs in the morning before exercise is the barometer which guides you in deciding how much work the horse is fit for. Both fore legs should be cool and hard (if they have had bandages on all night of course no one can tell whether they are naturally cool or not). If there is any tendency to puffiness or heat, those legs cannot be considered in really fit, hundred per cent condition.

Some horses' legs seem to be almost permanently puffy. Those horses are suffering from past overwork, or debility, which may take months to outgrow. They should not be called upon to do any really hard work, though they can quite easily do plenty of light exercise.

Sprains.—Nearly all sprains occur in the fore legs below the knee, and are connected with the suspensory ligament. It would be out of place for me in this chapter to go into the details of the various tendons and ligaments which operate a horse's leg; they can be studied in detail in any veterinary book. It will suffice for me to deal only with the sprain in general terms.

The treatment is simple. As long as there is inflammation, bathe the spot with hot water as often as possible and leave it to rest. Directly the inflammation has gone, massage repeatedly, exercise gently, and put the leg under the tap. *Don't* bandage; make massage your chief avenue to cure.

Foot Troubles.—The next most common troubles are to be found in the feet:

Thrush.—This is a rotting of the frog, due to constant dirt. The cure is, of course, to clean and apply antiseptics.

Laminitis.—This is sometimes called fever in the feet and is often due to too much banging on hard ground. The symptom is, that the horse seems to try to stand on his heels in order to relieve the pain in his toes. The cure is rest, with the shoes removed.

Contracted Heels.—Due to bad shoeing. The remedy is to remove the shoes.

Navicular.—This is a disease of the navicular or coffin bone in the horse's foot. The symptom is occasional unaccountable lameness and a tendency to stand upon the toes in the stable to relieve the weight on the heels. This is a serious matter and incurable.

Prick.—Sometimes a careless farrier will prick a horse. Directly this is discovered call in a veterinary surgeon at once, because unless the wound is properly attended to serious results may ensue.

Sidebones.—These are the two projecting bones on each side of the heel. They can become inflamed. The cure is rest.

Ringbone.—There are two ringbones, upper and lower. The upper one is half-way up the pastern, the other just above the coronet. Inflammation is due to jar. The cure is rest.

Splints.—These are little bony growths, which come on the cannon bone, and can be very troublesome. They are not really serious, and usually cease to be painful after a while. Sometimes, in order to accelerate their formation, a little local blister can be administered. If your horse goes lame, and you can find no cause for lameness, it may often be because a tiny splint, too small to be visible, is forming.

Greasy (or Cracked) Heels.—Heels that have not been properly cleaned or dried get sore. See that the heels are kept dry, apply lotion, and the trouble will disappear.

Overreach.—Horses, when galloping and jumping, especially in deep ground, are liable to strike their hind feet against their fore feet, and so cause a cut. This can be overcome, when persistent, by putting on rubber boots.

Windgalls, Thoroughpins, Bog Spavins.—These are soft lumps which come up on the side of the fetlock, or on the hocks. They are not a definite unsoundness, but they are unsightly. Pressure bandages are usually applied, and it is well also to massage, and reduce the exercise.

Spavins and Curbs.—These are ailments in the hocks. The treatment is rest, but it is best to call in a veterinary surgeon.

Brushing.—Horses, especially when weak, often rub one fetlock against the other foot. For this a boot should be put on. Sometimes the trouble can be lessened by careful shoeing.

Coughs, Colds, and Pink Eye.—These occur to the horse just the same as they do to man, and require much the same treatment. Keep the horse warm and out of draughts. Steamed hay in a nose-bag is often used to ease the lungs.

Vermin.—Horses coming in from grass, or from dirty stables, often have lice, ticks, botts, or ringworm in their skin. Ringworm is highly contagious, and the infected horse and his clothing must be segregated and a vet. called in.

Lampas.—Swollen gums, making it difficult for the horse to eat properly. Give cooling diet and gentle exercise.

Wind.—Horses sometimes go wrong in their wind. The reason for their doing so is a matter of much doubt and controversy. But it is a definite unsoundness. An operation can sometimes relieve it to such an extent as to be practically a cure.

Colic.—Very acute pains in the stomach. Caused by chill, or incorrect dieting. The horse keeps looking towards his stomach, or lies down. Remedy: keep warm, and hand-rub until the arrival of a veterinary surgeon.

Blistering and Firing.—These are drastic remedies. They are extremely painful, and should be applied only very rarely. Some people blister their horses constantly and needlessly. Rest, provided it is accompanied by either gentle exercise or massage, will work wonders for any sprain or enlargement. Firing should very seldom be resorted to by anyone who can afford to allow nature time to affect her own cure.

Mud Fever.—Often caused by washing mud off the legs after hunting. The mud should always be allowed to dry, when it can be removed by brushing in the usual way.

Note.—When in doubt as to the cause of lameness, remove the shoes.

XIX

THE PARTS OF A HORSE

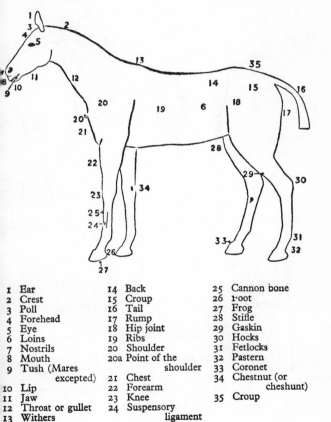

1 Ear	14 Back	25 Cannon bone
2 Crest	15 Croup	26 root
3 Poll	16 Tail	27 Frog
4 Forehead	17 Rump	28 Stifle
5 Eye	18 Hip joint	29 Gaskin
6 Loins	19 Ribs	30 Hocks
7 Nostrils	20 Shoulder	31 Fetlocks
8 Mouth	20a Point of the	32 Pastern
9 Tush (Mares	shoulder	33 Coronet
excepted)	21 Chest	34 Chestnut (or
10 Lip	22 Forearm	cheshunt)
11 Jaw	23 Knee	35 Croup
12 Throat or gullet	24 Suspensory	
13 Withers	ligament	

LOCALITIES OF AILMENTS

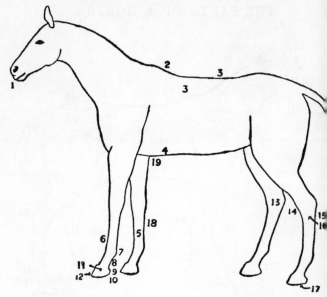

1	Lampas	10	Contracted heels
2	Rug gall	11	Navicular
3	Saddle gall	12	Laminitis
4	Girth gall	13	Thoroughpin
5	Splint	14	Spavin
6	Sprains { Suspensory ligament / Check ligament, etc.	15	Curb
		16	Bog spavin
7	Sesamoiditis	17	Thrush
8	Ringbone (upper and lower)	18	Speedy cut
9	Sidebone	19	Capped elbow

STABLE REQUISITES

WHEN starting a stable the following things are required:

Grooming Kit: Body brush, dandy brush, curry comb, comb, sponge, scraper, hoof-pick, rubbers and chamois leather, scissors, tail cutter.

Clothing: Day rug, night rug and blanket, bandages, tail cover (for travelling only), roller, knee-caps (for travelling only), hood (for travelling only), nose-bag, (for travelling only).

Stable Utensils: Log and head rope, head collar, wheelbarrow, pitchfork, shovel, basket; singeing lamp; twitch; corn bin, corn measure and basket; pillar chains, clipping machines, drenching horn, eye fringe (for flies).

Cleaning Materials: Soap, dubbing, polishing paste, tin of grease, rubbers, burnisher.

Saddlery: Double bridle, saddle, snaffle, stirrup irons, girths, standing martingale.

HOW TO DESCRIBE A HORSE

IN describing a horse, the colour is usually put first, then the sex and age, then the height, and finally any markings which describe it distinctively.

An 'aged' horse is one over 7 years. The reason for this term is that, up to 7, the age can be accurately determined by the markings on the tops of the teeth; but as the horse grows older, the exact year of birth becomes less certain, and unless one knows from other sources what the real age is, it is safer to call him 'aged'. The age of racehorses is always reckoned from the first of January, so that late foals are often useless for racing for this reason alone. With other horses, it is usual to reckon the age from the first of April, which approximates more closely to the real date of birth.

As a horse's markings are nearly always white, it is considered unnecessary to use the term 'white': 'stocking off hind,' 'sock near fore' is enough. It is also useful to remember that whenever a horse gets a sore, the hair on the spot usually turns white; many descriptions of markings, therefore, represent past rubs—for example, 'trace marks', 'collar marks', 'saddle marks'. Most horses have some white on their faces. The 'star' is most common. When the star runs down the nose in a thin line it is called a 'race'; when it is in a broad shape it is a 'blaze'; a little mark is a 'snip'.

The following are typical descriptions:

Chestnut mare (ch. m.), 15·1, aged, star and blaze, both hind fetlocks.

Or:

Bay gelding (b. g.), 16·2, 5 years, faint star, saddle marks, off fore fetlock.

(1)

(2)

(3)

STUDIES OF THE LEAP

PLATE XXII **102**

(1)

(2)

(3)

STUDIES OF THE LEAP

Then, as to height: a 'hand' is 4 inches, and it is well to remember that 15 hands is exactly 5 feet. 15·1 equals therefore 5 feet 4 inches; and so on. The height is taken from the highest part of the withers.

The following is a table of colours with their sub-divisions:

Chestnut	bright	Yellow.
	dark	Bronze.
	liver	The colour of a piece of liver.
Bay		Bright brown.
Brown		Mahogany.
Grey	dappled	Wavy spots.
	flea-bitten	A lot of small spots.
	iron	Like flint.
White		Rather rare; confined as a rule to very old horses; must not be confused with grey.
Roan	strawberry blue red	A mixed colour.
Piebald		Black and white in patches.
Skewbald		Chestnut (or other colour) and white in patches.
Dun		Khaki.
Black		Black.
Cream		A light dun.

When you are not sure of a horse's colour, look at the muzzle: that is the sure guide, because that never changes; the other parts of the coat do change, according to the time of year.

XXIII
STABLE TRICKS

1. *GETTING LOOSE.*—A difficult thing to cure. The best preventive is a strong throat lash to the head collar, buckled tightly, and a strong chain.

2. *Weaving.*—This is a restless habit of worrying the head from side to side. It is purely nervous, and the best treatment is sympathetic handling both in the stable and out.

3. *Pawing.*—Also due to nervousness. Do not, as some people suggest, shackle the horse; try to overcome his nervousness by quiet treatment.

4. *Eating Bedding.*—If obvious remedies, such as changing the hay, will not answer, then bed upon peat moss. Do not muzzle.

5. *Crib-biting and Wind-sucking.*—Often produced through loneliness or lack of exercise. If the horse cannot be broken of these habits, endeavour to remove all projecting parts from the box and cover those which cannot be removed, so that they are too wide for the teeth to seize.

6. *Night-kicking.*—Difficult to cure. Try to discover and remove the cause.

7. *Capped Elbows.*—Caused by the shoe when lying down.

8. *Capped Hocks.*—Caused by rubbing the hocks against the walls of the stall or box.

XXIV
A FEW STABLE EXPRESSIONS

'OFF side.' The right side.

'Near side.' The left side.

'Standing over.' Standing with knees bent.

'Back in the knee', or 'calf-kneed'. Weak-kneed.

'Tied in below the knee.' When the measurement round the leg just below the knee is much less than that lower down.

'On the leg.' Long-legged.

'Flat-sided.' Having ribs that are too oval-shaped.

'Well ribbed up.' The opposite of flat-sided: round ribs and a short back.

'Goose-rumped.' Short of muscle on the top of the rump.

'Herring-gutted.' Short of measurement in the loin.

'Short of bone', 'good bone'. The 'bone' of a horse is measured just below the knee. 'Good bone' is $8\frac{1}{2}$ to 9 inches. 'Short (or light) of bone' is, say, 8 inches.

'Hairy-heeled.' Because cart horses have hairy heels (or feather), it is the sign of a badly bred horse to have much hair round the fetlocks.

'Roach-backed.' Shaped with a prominent spinal cord, as many walers (Australian horses).

'Cow-hocked.' With hocks that turn inwards.

'Sickle-hocked.' With hocks shaped like a sickle.

'Ewe-necked.' With a neck that looks as if it had been put on backwards, like that of a ewe.

'Dishing.' Moving with a splay action.

'Winding.' Moving with a winding in and out action.

'Brushing.' Rubbing one fetlock against another.

'Split up.' Undeveloped below the tail.

'Nothing in front', or 'straight-shouldered'. With bad shoulders.

'Good frontispiece', or 'lots in front of you', or 'good rein'. Good sloping shoulders.

'Star gazer.' A horse that carries his head too high.

'Nappy.' Inclined to 'refuse' very suddenly.

'Yawing.' Reaching with the mouth and pulling the reins through the rider's fingers.

'One-sided.' Having a mouth that is harder on one side than on the other.

'Nut cracker.' A horse that grinds his teeth.

'Good doer.' A horse that always eats well.

'Forging', or 'clicking'. Striking the hind foot against the fore foot when trotting.

'Refuser.' A horse that will not jump.

'Fiddle-headed.' With an ugly head.

'Grunts under the stick.' If a horse is slightly touched in the wind he will 'grunt' if frightened by the sight of the stick.

'Long-tailed horses.' Usually means racehorses or thorough-breds.

'Cock-tails.' Usually means half-breeds (now rather out of date).

Wind Troubles:

'A roarer.' A horse that is very bad in the wind.

'A whistler.' A horse that is very slightly touched in the wind.

'A grunter.' See 'Grunts under the stick'.

'Peacocky.' With a high and useless action.

'Stringhalt.' The nervous raising of the hind legs very high when at the walk.

'A good hunter.' Means, for sale purposes, that the horse has been hunted, is capable of being hunted, and sound in wind and eyes. Without this designation in a sale catalogue your hunter will not fetch much.

'In the book.' A thoroughbred horse whose birth and parentage have been registered.

SADDLERY

Snaffle. A plain bit, with usually a large round ring on each side.

Bit (or curb). A bit with side-pieces, and a curb chain.

Port (high or low). The bent part in the mouthpiece of the bit.

Curb chain. The chain attached to the bit.

Cheeks. The side-pieces of the bit.

Brow-band. The strap over the horse's forehead.

Throat lash. The strap going round the horse's cheek.

Nose-band. The strap going round the nose.

Cheek pieces. The straps on each side of the bridle.

Double bridle. A bridle composed of bit and snaffle.

Pelham. A bit bridle with two reins.

Martingale. The strap that checks a horse's head as it rises. There are three kinds:

Standing. With the strap fixed to the nose-band.

Running. With rings that go over either the snaffle or the bit rein.

Irish. A short circular strap which goes over all the reins, in front of the horse's throat.

Breastplate. Straps which are fixed to the saddle and to a neck strap to keep the saddle from slipping back.

Neck strap. A part of the martingale.

Then come the Saddle, the Girths, the Stirrup leathers, Stirrup irons, which need no further description.

The metal loops on the saddle, for attaching breastplate or sandwich case to, are called 'D's'.

XXV

HOW TO FIT SADDLERY

The Snaffle should rest in, without crinkling, the corners of the mouth.

The Bit should rest about one inch above the tush of a horse or two inches above the corner tooth of a mare.

The Nose-band should admit of two fingers between it and the horse's nose, and two fingers between it and the projecting cheek-bone.

The Throat Lash should be just tight enough to prevent the bridle from slipping over the horse's ears.

The Martingale:
  Running—the rings should reach the top of the withers.
  Standing—should be long enough to check the abnormal and give full play to every normal movement.

The Girths should be tight enough to admit of one finger. They are usually too tight.

The Curb Chain should lie flat upon the chin groove. With the usual large links, 13 make nearly always the correct length. If there are more than 13 in your chain, put the last links on first and loop up on the near side only; if there are 15, there can be one spare link on each side.

The Breastplate if worn (it is quite useless), should admit of a hand's breadth between it and the horse's shoulder.

The Stirrup Leathers. The spare ends should not be tucked into the buckle, because that makes readjustment from the saddle too difficult, but should be turned back under the double leather and pulled up horizontal. The buckle should be flush with the side bar and resting flat against it.

XXVI

SCHOOLING

THE object of schooling a horse is to make him obedient to the leg and rein.

The results of schooling are that a horse acquires a good mouth, that he is so balanced as to use all his limbs to the best advantage, and that he is so much under control that he will go anywhere the rider wishes with exactness, at any pace required, at any time.

These are advantages worth working for, and when you have once ridden a perfectly schooled horse you will never again want to ride one that is not. In this chapter I do not propose to deal with the early handling of a youngster—longeing and long rein work—but to explain what to do with a horse you have just bought.

It is not necessary to have expensive apparatus, such as closed riding schools or jumping lanes, or even open manèges; as long as you have a piece of land which is flat and where the going is generally good, you have all that is necessary. You will need no special appliances: no spurs of any sort, not even blunt ones; even your stick will be necessary only as an assistant to your legs, to be applied sometimes firmly but never painfully: you will need nothing in fact, but your own strong legs, light hands, and voice.

The first rule of schooling is to see that your lessons are apportioned equally to both sides of the horse. Whatever you do to the right, you must do equally to the left. It is difficult, but very important, to keep your horse 'ambi-pedestric' (if I may be allowed to coin a word): that is, equally exercised on the left rein as on the right. In order to save repetition, I shall not refer to this point again, but shall deal with the right side only, leaving my readers to understand that precisely the same rules apply to the left side; all the exercises must be carried out on a 'fifty-fifty' basis.

Let us now begin our exercises.

MOUNTING

First teach your horse to stand still while you mount him, not moving until you give the definite order. This can best be done by mounting from a block. Tranquillity must be the theme of your schooling, so see that you begin on the right note.

TURN TO THE RIGHT

There are three turns:

1. On the centre.
2. On the forehand.
3. On the hock.

These are important because much develops therefrom.

The turn on the centre is easy. It is the normal way. Here the horse pivots on his centre, with the fore and hind feet both circling round it. The 'aid' for this is a light feeling of the right rein and a slight pressure of the right leg, which should be slightly drawn back.

For the turn on the forehand, the horse pivots on his fore leg, the hind legs circling round it. The aid is the same as for the centre turn, but much more pronounced. The right leg must be more strongly used and drawn farther back. The right rein must be drawn more tightly. If necessary the whip can be used to tap the horse on the right quarter.

The third turn, on the hock, is more difficult. Here the horse pivots upon his right hind leg, which does not move. How to do this depends a good deal on the horse. Normally, the rider's right leg is put back to check the movement of the quarters, and the left leg is put a little forward to push the horse's shoulder round. If, however, the horse begins to move his quarters to the left, then the rider's left leg must check this with a backward pressure, and the whip must be used to tap the horse's left shoulder. The left rein is used to keep the horse's head straight. (This is an early application of what is called 'neck reining').

These are the three turns to the right, and they should be constantly practised. If your horse gets bewildered and starts to rein back or otherwise to try to evade the lesson, push him forward at a walk and start again.

The next exercise is to circle at the walk. Here we must see first of all that the horse makes a true circle: not an elongated obloid with its apex towards home or to another horse; but a perfect circle. The head must be inclined inwards; but care should be taken to see that the horse does not lean inwards, but makes the circle by bending his ribs. He must go round the circle shaped like a bow, with his hind legs following exactly in the track of the fore legs. This will supple his neck and ribs. Simple though it appears, there is a great deal more in it than one might suppose; it is a very important exercise and should be done constantly.

The next exercise is to do the same thing on two tracks. Put the horse round your circle, this time feeling strongly the right leg and rein, so as to turn his head in towards the centre of the circle, and with the pressure of the leg force the hind legs out. In this way the circle is made on two tracks, the fore legs making a small circle and the hind legs a larger circle. This exercise is most easily done round a tree.

Then we have the second way, on two tracks, where the hind legs make the small, and the fore legs the bigger, circle. To do this you must get in the open again, and, by applying the same aids as you did when making the turn on the hock, force the horse's forehand over either by advancing the left leg or by tapping on the left shoulder. In this exercise the horse should come round with his back and body straight.

It will now be an easy matter to get the 'half passage'.

In this the horse puts his feet one in front of the other, thus gaining ground to the front and to the right at the same time. You must be careful to see that the horse does not turn his head to the left; if anything, he should look a trifle to the right. The aid is to press the left leg, drawn back firmly against the horse's back ribs, and feel the right rein, so as to keep the head straight. The exercise is of no value unless the horse brings his left hind leg well over in front of the right hind leg, and unless the general direction is strictly maintained. If it is done, for example, when walking down a lane, the whole line of the horse's body must always be kept parallel with the direction of the lane. Getting sideways must be checked at once, as must any tendency to rein back and so evade the exercise.

REIN BACK

We must now teach our horse to rein back. The 'aid' is to raise his head slightly, and then to close both legs firmly, and immediately after feel both reins. But before the horse understands what is wanted, this may be difficult. You must get his nose down, before attempting it, because if the nose is in the air, no result will be obtained. In obstinate cases as assistant may tap the horse's fore legs to help him to understand what is required. But directly the horse does understand, it becomes a very easy exercise and one which, after a while, can be accomplished by the lightest possible touch on the mouth. With the exception of the rein back and the turns, all these exercises should now be done at the trot.

Now, in trotting, the rider sinks in the saddle as either the rear fore or the off fore hoof touches the ground. These are known as the off and near diagonal. In schooling it is very necessary that the horse should learn to carry the rider upon either diagonal with equal facility. It is easy to see which diagonal you are on as you sink in the saddle: look down and see on which side the fore foot meets the ground at that moment. When trotting round to the right, it is well to be on the right diagonal. When you want to change from one diagonal to the other, you nearly stand in your stirrup for a half-beat and continue sinking and rising as before. You will find that that is all that is necessary to change. If you want to start off from the walk upon some given diagonal, watch the horse's shoulder. When that shoulder is back, then break into the trot, and rise at the same moment. You will find you are on the diagonal you meant to be. Many horses have never been taught to carry their riders thus, and are awkward to begin with. They feel uncomfortable, and will be constantly making some excuse to put you back on to the accustomed side, such as making little shies, or breaking. Sometimes it takes many weeks to get a horse equal-sided in this. Therefore keep on changing when doing your circles. Be on the right diagonal when going to the right and on the left diagonal when going to the left.

In trotting, keep the horse's head well up, and so get a cadenced motion with propulsion from the hock. Do not let the horse trot with his nose stuck out. This produces an unbalanced 'run .

THE CANTER

Having done all these exercises at the walk and trot, the same must be done at the canter, on one track and then on two tracks. To get a horse to canter upon the right leg it will be necessary to get him to strike off with that leg. To do this, exert a strong pressure of the left leg, lean a little back, and very momentarily feel the left rein; but directly the horse breaks off, the right rein should be used, because it is of great importance that the head should be slightly turned to that side, and to see that the horse does not lean over, but circles by bending his ribs.

When you have got your horse to canter correctly in the circle on both reins, it will become necessary to make the 'change' or the 'figure of eight'. First of all give a definite check, so that the animal knows that something is going to happen; without this check you cannot possibly be sure of his making the change correctly. He will probably change in front instead of behind, and that is a bad fault. It is so easy to change a horse in front that the rider should concentrate on the hind leg. When you come to the centre of your figure 8, give this check, bend the body over to the other side, apply the aid with the leg, and the horse will soon learn to make the change correctly.

There is so much in this exercise that few horses will learn to do it perfectly correctly for several weeks. But when it is done properly it is a very attractive thing to see.

The next exercise to practise is the canter from the rein back. First rein back a few strides, then by a very firm pressure of both legs, and by yielding both reins, make the horse break off with a canter. This alone is not very difficult; what is difficult is to get him to break into a canter upon whatever leg you desire. It is done by a strong pressure of the left leg drawn back, to make the horse strike off with the right leg.

The next stage is to get him to change on the straight. First put him into a canter on the right leg, and make him half-passage to the right, then a slight check, change, and half-passage to the left. You must remember to keep your direction all the time. After the horse understands what is wanted you must then do it to a pattern: say, twelve paces to the right and then twelve paces to the left. When he can do this correctly, reduce it to six paces each way, then four, and finally two.

When you have reached this stage you can say to yourself that you have got a really nicely schooled horse.

Throughout your schooling remember these rules:

Be quiet and patient.

Never fight your horse. If he doesn't understand, use your ingenuity to try to make the lesson easier.

Stick to patterns as far as possible; they make it easier for the horse to know what is wanted.

Don't allow your horse to get either nervous or fretful, but make him enjoy his lessons as far as possible.

JUMPING

In schooling horses to jump, there are many factors which apply only to the particular horse we have in hand. It is therefore not possible to lay down a definite curriculum for every horse. But it is possible to frame a few guiding principles.

Any horse can be schooled to jump well without expensive appliances. It is not necessary to erect a series of formidable obstacles. With a little ingenuity a great deal can be done at no cost at all. Few realize this, however. A man once complained to me that he had nowhere where he could school his horse. The time of year was August; and when I made up for him several excellent jumps out of the sheafs of corn which stood all round his house he was very agreeably surprised. Make the best use you can of local conditions; it is wonderful how much you will be able to do. A fallen tree trunk, for example, is excellent; a few fallen boughs can be made up into something; old beer barrels are admirable; and wattle hurdles of different sizes (with smooth tops) can be made up into almost any kind of jump. Try to make your jumps portable, because, especially in winter, one spot may get poached and useless. Wings should be avoided; make your horse go straight at a fence by the use of your legs; wings are efficacious only when the training is upon unsound lines. Always make your horse jump a fence at exactly the place you mean him to—it is a good plan to mark the spot with a piece of paper. This may be called 'bull's-eye' jumping, and it is very interesting to see how often you can get full marks for your effort.

Let us now consider the following list of rules:

1. Never jump a larger fence until your horse can jump the smaller one perfectly.
2. Never use either whip or spur, as punishment.
3. Avoid excitement. If your horse gets too worked up, go back to easier jumps.
4. When he jumps, be sure you give him a free head and a free loin. When schooling an inexperienced horse I strongly advise the rider to hold on to the neck strap; this makes a certainty of not interfering with his head, no matter how awkwardly he jumps.
5. Make him jump straight and exactly where you mean to go.
6. Discourage the putting in of a short stride before jumping. This shows lack of confidence.
7. Jump often and daily, when the fences are small, in order to work up the muscles and to instil assurance; but over big fences jump seldom.
8. Work for complete tranquillity. Try to get your horse to stand motionless and straight in front of the fence, about 40 feet away from it. Break from the stand into a canter upon a previously determined leg. Three increasing strides and over. Pull up 40 feet away. Be motionless. Turn on the hock. Be motionless again. Then, from the stand, break into a canter upon the other leg, and carry on as before. Your horse should be able to jump with equal facility off either leg, and remain on it after landing.
9. See that your horse jumps with lowered head and rounded back.
10. Do not jump your horse until he has been schooled and is obedient to the leg and rein. Most horses set their jaws on the approach and so make delicate control an impossibility.

11. If your horse is a sticky jumper give him width, as opposed to height, to jump. If he is too free give him in and out fences, or even four or five in quick succession about 15 feet apart (according to his scope).

12. Do not use furze jumps. They are disagreeable to a horse and make him fret.

13. If a horse knocks down the rail, do not punish him. He did not do it because he was careless but because he was either off his balance, had not used his hocks sufficiently, or was not sufficiently muscled up. Remember that a perfectly balanced and muscularly fit horse will clear big obstacles with ease. It is your job to put him at the fence correctly.

14. Do not jump a horse until you have done some suppling exercises. This is important.

15. Remember it is natural to horses to touch the top rail lightly. We cannot abuse them for it, but hope by more development to make their loins stronger.

16. If your horse is very sluggish, there is probably something amiss.

17. If he refuses unexpectedly, search for the cause. The ground is probably too slippery, or he may have a pinching saddle or other discomfort.

18. Jump as much off the near fore as off the off for.

19. A horse should not take off much nearer than six feet away from any fence higher than two feet. If he does, put down a low rail in front to prevent it.

20. As your horse gets more amenable, it is a good practice to put him at obstacles of less and less length, until you succeed in getting him to jump over, let us say, a sawn tree trunk no longer than three feet. This shows complete obedience, and is most useful in the hunting field.

21. Teach him to jump his fences at whatever pace you

     ask. But be sure of his jumping them slowly and collectedly first; speed can be attained easily.

22. Finally, remember it is neither necessary nor wise to try to attain mastery on any special occasion. Because a horse refuses the fence you put him at, it is not necessary to force him to jump it all that day; another day will be much better.

With these simple rules, any horse can be trained to jump in good style, whether for the hunting field, the show-ring or the race-course, in the quietest, and therefore the most effective way.

As an example of schooling, Plate XXIII shows a horse doing a figure of 8 at the canter, and jumping a fence at the gallop. He is being ridden in reins of brown paper, which in order to make it more conclusive have been cut in half and joined together by a single thread. This is more clearly seen in Fig. 1 than in Fig. 2. This is a standard that nearly every horse could be brought to by careful work and by the correct application of the rider's legs, and it is the goal at which to aim. It signifies absolute obedience and control by the lightest touch, and the horse, as can be seen by his ears, is happy and contented.

(1) THE FIGURE OF 8

(2) THE JUMP

A SCHOOLED HORSE IN PAPER REINS

XXVII

'VICE' IN HORSES

I FEAR I have to use this objectionable word 'vice' because there is no other in our language to express the troubles that arise in schooling horses. Personally, I am convinced that there is no native 'vice' in horses, and that practically every difficulty is the outcome of injudicious handling and can be removed by sympathetic treatment. The fact, however, remains that when a horse 'plays up' or shows either nervousness or resentment, it is described as 'vice'.

Of course, there are horses in whom some habit has become confirmed, and it seems as if gentleness were no solution. But we must remember that if a horse has been expecting trouble for say ten years, a week's kindness will hardly balance the account in his mind. Owners who have horses like these, finding kindness does not, apparently, work, give up that plan, and either take to severity or sell the horse. Thus we find so many people who have what they call 'exceptions', which, when we come to look into them, we usually find to be no exception at all.

Jibbing. Let us suppose that you have bought a horse which possesses or acquires the habit of 'jibbing'—refusing to go forward. Let me say straight away that with such a horse it is the worst possible policy to be severe. Very many people will tell you to put on a pair of sharp spurs, but I urge all my readers to do no such thing. The best and, I think, the only cure is patience. The fault is in no way a vicious one. It is due largely to nervousness, and might be compared to stammering in a child. We would never hit a child who stammered: why should we hit or otherwise punish a horse that jibs? If, after you have urged a horse on with your knees and legs, he continues to stop, be very calm. Speak to him, pat him. Never show him the whip. (In fact it is better to leave your whip at home.) If he continues to 'jib', dismount; pat him again and try to lead him If he refuses—wait. Pat him again. If possible walk him round in a circle. Do everything you can to quieten his nerves. You may have to wait quite a time before he will go on. But don't let that worry you. He will go on eventually, and each day the trouble will get less and less. I once had what is called by most people 'a confirmed jibber'. I was told that the animal was so bad that it could never be cured. And certainly the cure took longer than any other I have known; but in four months the mare was fit to go anywhere.

Rearing. This, once it has become a habit, is difficult to stop. Many people advocate all kinds of severe measures. Breaking a bottle of warm water over the ears is sometimes suggested! Or pulling the horse backwards! Needless to say, I am strongly opposed to any such expedients. It is best, in my opinion, not to try to cure the rearing itself, but to remove the cause of it. A horse rears, generally, by way of expostulation; he wishes to show that he dislikes the task which he is either being asked to perform, or which he expects to be asked to perform. Hence, it is best to make his exercises easier, and show him that he has no cause for complaint. But sometimes a horse will rear because a bad rider worries him with conflicting indications. Here the cure is obvious, although it may be difficult to execute. But no matter what our difficulties, let us remember that rearing is nearly always a protest, not a vice.

Kicking. Some horses, especially those that have had sore backs at some time or another, develop the bad habit of kicking. The best way to cure this is to keep the horse's head up as much as possible when you think he is likely to do it, to rate him with the voice, jab him on the mouth, and put the stick firmly along his shoulder. But directly you notice the habit beginning, examine the animal's back carefully for an incipient sore.

Running away. This is another habit which some people call a 'vice'. But how can it be? Horses don't *want* to gallop 'all out'. No, indeed! They run away because they have been ridden badly. Left alone, they would soon stop, trot back to their stable, or begin to eat grass. How to cure the habit is a little difficult to explain. But if such a horse came to my stable, this is what I should do. I should examine his mouth: and probably I should find it very sore and swollen. If it were too bad to ride, I should exercise the animal on the longeing rein attached to the head collar, until the mouth was healed, or ride him in a 'Hackamore'. This would be doing three things: it would be giving the horse the necessary exercise, saving his mouth, and helping to flex his neck muscles. When he was ready to be ridden again, I should ride him only at very slow paces, and describe small circles. If he wished to go faster than I wanted, or resisted my hand, I would bring him back to the walk and narrow the circle. I would then soon commence the exercises I have described in the preceding chapter, and, in a few weeks, the horse would be cantering along on a loose rein, without excitement, and going exactly where he was asked.

This is no occupation, however, for beginners, as it not only takes a good deal of time but plenty of experience. If, therefore, you are a young rider, and find your horse pulls you so much that you can't hold him, it is better to get rid of him and try something easier to start with.

But be sure of this:

Putting a more severe bit in the horse's mouth will *not* cure the trouble.

XXVIII

SOME HUNTING RULES FOR BEGINNERS

1. TAKE care about your turn out. Nothing 'gives away' a novice more than eccentricity of dress.

2. See that your hunting-crop is strong enough to open and hold a heavy gate. A little 'lady-like' one is merely ridiculous.

3. Find out what the 'cap' is, and have it ready for the secretary when he asks for it. It is pleasanter for you to offer it to him, rather than that he should have to run after you for it.

4. If you are joining the hunt as a regular subscriber, get an introduction as soon as possible to the master. If you are only out for the day this will not be necessary.

5. Unless you are quite sure that your horse is quiet with hounds, keep away from the hounds as far as possible at the meet.

6. If hounds pass you in a roadway turn your horse's head towards them to avoid the possibility of kicking one.

7. If your horse kicks at other horses, you must put a piece of red ribbon in his tail as a warning. Do not think, however, that this is all you need do. You must avoid getting into a crowd and do all you can to prevent anyone being kicked.

8. During a run, keep well back from hounds, in order to give them a chance to hunt.

9. When they are drawing a cover don't make a noise: keep quite still.

10. Remember that hounds often turn down a hedge-row, so if you are close to them do not jump the fence too

soon, or you may jump on one. Don't be too eager or enthusiastic to jump the fence first.

11. If you see a fox breaking cover unobserved by any whipper-in or hunt servant, don't holloa 'gone away' until he has really gone away, otherwise he may turn back. To count twenty before holloaing was the motto of 'Jorrocks', and it was a very sound one too.

12. Don't gallop over seeds if you can help it. Remember that every footmark on grass seeds kills. This does not apply to wheat, but it is best, nevertheless, to avoid all seeds if you can.

13. Don't gallop over roots; every bruise is bad for them, and you can do much damage.

14. If you are the last, see that you close the gates, especially if there are cattle about.

15. Make every effort to avoid doing damage. If your horse is a bad jumper, the hunting-field is not the place to school him in.

16. When your horse has had enough, it is time to go home, whatever the hour may be. Don't think it is 'sporting' to stop out on a tired horse.

17. Don't interfere with straggling hounds. The thong of your crop is not for that purpose.

18. If you see sheep or cattle making for an open gate, do all you can to stop them, by cracking your whip, etc. (If, however, you haven't practised this at home it is better not to try it in the hunting-field.)

19. Don't jump unnecessary places; a fence should be regarded as an obstacle to avoid rather than a 'joy' jump.

20. Never 'cut in'. Always wait your turn at a gap. It is better to lose a place or two than to jump before you should.

21. When you have finished, endeavour to get your horse back to his stable as soon as you can. A steady trot

home is better than a dawdle. But don't go home fast: and don't bring your horse in hot.

22. There is no harm in allowing your horse to water on the way home, so long as you keep him warm by walking on quietly afterwards.

23. Don't ride your horse in bandages.

24. Don't put a coloured brow-band on the bridle.

25. A hunt is not a steeplechase. It doesn't matter who jumps a fence first. The wiser ones jump it after a lead.

26. Unless you know the country well, don't try to take your own line; to do this is to ask for trouble.

27. When galloping down a muddy lane, try not to splash people.

28. Don't let gates slam in people's faces; hold them open until they get up, if you can.

29. If some one has dismounted to open a gate for you, see that he is mounted again before you gallop off.

30. Don't talk to the hunt servants unnecessarily. They have their own work to do.

31. If you see wire in a fence, or a rabbit hole, or other danger, shout out 'ware' (pronounced 'war', as in tug-of-war), 'wire', 'ware holes', etc.

32. Don't forget to wear a hat-guard, and to have string gloves under the saddle for use in wet weather.

33. Don't forget to look to your girths before moving off.

34. Ladies should remember that all jewellery, except a tie-pin, must be left at home.

35. When you come to a gate, put your crop into the hand on the side of the hinges.

36. If you have a red coat, wear it. Do not think that pink coats are for regular members only. But do not put on the hunt button or collar until you have paid the full yearly subscription, or until you have permission to do so.

37. Don't 'lark' over fences on the way home.

38. Don't jump a fence close to a tree with branches.
39. When going under an archway always bend down much lower than you think necessary.
40. When going through woodland, don't, in order to be polite, hang on to branches to help the man behind, for this does more harm than good.
41. Always give a cheery 'good night!' to farmers and farm hands whom you meet on the way home.

XXIX

CONCLUSION

THIS book, comprehends a wide range within its title, *The Art of Riding*, and as I bring my last chapter to its conclusion, I realize how difficult is the task I set myself and how superficially I have been able only to touch upon subjects which in themselves are each worthy of a book. But I console myself with the thought that lengthy dissertations, however ably written, are seldom read, and lie as monuments to well-meant but wasted endeavour on the shelves of many an unopened library.

Therefore, bearing in mind the sub-title, 'A Textbook for Beginners and Others', my endeavour has been to place the more salient matters on horse-management, riding, and horsemanship before you in short and simple chapters to refer to or to commit to memory.

I make no pretence to have produced a comprehensive work. All I hope is that I may have interested some riders enough to make them want to know more and to realize how much there is to learn in what is possibly the most fascinating of all studies—The Art of Riding.